D1736304

Race, Justice and American Intellectual Traditions

J Kegley
April 1
_2018_

Stuart Rosenbaum

Race, Justice and American Intellectual Traditions

palgrave
macmillan

Stuart Rosenbaum
Baylor University
Waco, TX, USA

ISBN 978-3-319-76197-8   ISBN 978-3-319-76198-5   (eBook)
https://doi.org/10.1007/978-3-319-76198-5

Library of Congress Control Number: 2018933047

Cover illustration: © nemesis2207/Fotolia.co.uk

Printed on acid-free paper

This Palgrave Pivot imprint is published by the registered company
Springer International Publishing AG part of Springer Nature
The registered company address is: Gewerbestrasse 11, 6330 Cham, Switzerland

CONTENTS

CHAPTER 1

Prologue

Abstract Ideas have consequences, and ideas have origins. Origins are at least as important as consequences, and sometimes more important, as the origin of the automobile illustrates. Likewise, moral ideas have origins equally significant for their content, as does the idea of justice. Our traditional European ideas of justice include the foundations of slavery and genocide. Only indigenous ideas of justice avoid those foundations.

Keywords Race · Native American · Slavery · Henry Ford
Twenty-first-century racism

Ideas have consequences and ideas have origins. In thinking that ideas have consequences, we acknowledge the importance of what follows from them. In acknowledging that ideas have origins, we acknowledge the importance of those origins. But why are origins of ideas important?

Origins are important because they reveal particulars and contexts and alternatives. The idea of the automobile, for example, originated in a context where people moved about in vehicles drawn by animals; those vehicles were not self-moving. In that context, "self-mobility" was not possible. Combine that pre-automobile context with some inventions, along with the creativity of Henry Ford and his precursors, and you have the origin of self-mobility—*auto*mobiles.

© The Author(s) 2018
S. Rosenbaum, *Race, Justice and American Intellectual Traditions*,
https://doi.org/10.1007/978-3-319-76198-5_1

Seeing the origin of the automobile, and the idea of it, draws attention also to elaborations of that idea. A "flying car," for example, represents the intersection of the ideas of an automobile and an airplane. Ideas, coupled with contexts and human creativity, have cultural consequences. The idea of the automobile originated in a specific context, and apart from that context, the idea might not have appeared. Automobiles originated in the Western, industrial world, not elsewhere. In addition, the origins we know might have produced different results and different cultural consequences.

Henry Ford, for example, was famous for saying about his cars, "People can have any color they want, so long as it's black." If Ford had prevailed, automobiles might not have become the colorful appliances we see about us today. One might elaborate particulars and contexts of origin for many ideas—indeed for *all* ideas. And one might explore as well questions naturally associated with the idea that ideas have origins. Why, for example, did automobiles originate only in the Western, industrial world? Why did Henry Ford's preference for black automobiles not dominate for long in the commercial production of automobiles? Why did the Chinese or the Indians not produce automobiles? All such questions must be answered in terms of the particulars and contexts that give rise to ideas and their uses in particular places and times. What about ideas of morality? Do they have origins? Do they have particular contexts wherein they arise and function?

JUSTICE

All ideas have origins, and one may understand ideas of morality by attending carefully to the particulars and contexts in which they originate and have their home. The idea of justice is of special interest in the contemporary American world.

The American world is morally complex in specific ways we barely acknowledge and rarely mention. American history is, from contemporary perspectives, rife with immoralities. The genocide we inflicted on Native Americans for five centuries, we rarely acknowledge. The slavery we practiced for four centuries, we believe we have transcended. Was it *just* for our forebears to kill Native Americans and to take for themselves and us the lands those Natives had lived on and with for thousands of years before we crossed the Atlantic? Was slavery a *just*—or at least not an *unjust*—institution?

We *now* know the answers to these questions, and we believe we have put aside the immoralities of our American ancestors. But the trauma of those immoralities continues to shape our American world. So perhaps we have not really gotten away from those injustices? Perhaps they continue to shape our lives?

RACE

The most prominent expression of the injustice that continues to shape our lives is racism. Native Americans now live on reservations far from population centers and are little in our awareness. Black Americans, however, live among white Americans, and the legacy of slavery and of the century and a half following it lives on in our American world.

Twenty-first-century racism is the long shadow of America's 500 years of racist white supremacy. Specific parts of that long shadow are contents of the following chapters. Black "criminality" and police shootings of black men and boys are some parts of that shadow that are important in what follows. But part of that 500-year legacy of racism and white supremacy, and part of that long shadow are the moral ideas interwoven with it.

All moral ideas in our contemporary world have origins and histories. Understanding those origins and histories enables us to see alternatives. Seeing alternatives to our moral ideas can empower us in ways we seldom imagine.

Seeing how Platonism is writ into our moral ideas enables us to think alternatives to those Platonist dimensions of our thought. Seeing how Enlightenment ideas of morality are embedded in our moral thinking enables us to think beyond those ideas. Seeing how our understanding of justice has specific historical roots enables us to think beyond those roots.

The point of this book is to reveal some historical foundations of contemporary moral thinking—and in particular of our thought about justice. Our American racism is intricately interwoven with the historical roots of our thought about justice.

Plato, the Enlightenment, our Constitution and our long, messy history of racism need to be revealed in their naked collusion. We need to see our racist history and our moral traditions as intimately woven together. Only seeing how our moral traditions enforce our racism, and also how our racism reinforces our moral thinking can enable us to see a more constructive world beyond the racism deeply embedded in our lives.

This book is a partial unmasking of the moral traditions that enable and perpetuate our racism. Part I (*Our Problem, Our Justice, Our Past*) is an argument that our large Western moral traditions are racist. Five primary chapters elaborate Western sources of our moral traditions and a sixth summarizes those five.

Part II (*Our Problem, Our Responsibility, Our Future*) finds a constructive alternative to our moral traditions rooted in an indigenous, American moral tradition that holds the promise of freedom from our racism. Four chapters bring us into a contemporary world that needs our indigenous moral traditions.

* * *

A note about my use of the term "indigenous." I use the term more expansively than is customary, and I hope doing so is not objectionable to those accustomed to using it in a more restrictive way. The normal restrictive way of using the term constrains its application to Native Americans or First Peoples or to what originates solely with them. My more expansive use of the term allows it to include perspectives of non-European and still American origin. Thus W.E.B. DuBois and John Dewey, since their perspectives on matters moral, religious and social do have deep roots in the American, non-European world are legitimate representatives of indigenous thought. And I believe significant benefits follow from this more expansive use of "indigenous."

One benefit of the more expansive use is that connections between genuinely (restricted use) "indigenous" peoples and the (expansive use) "indigenous" perspectives I see in DuBois and Dewey become stronger together, and more distinctive in contrast to the European perspectives I claim are racist. Scott Pratt has elaborated this connection nicely in his *Native Pragmatism*, and I would be happy to claim Pratt's imprimatur for the claims I make here about the indigenous—and pragmatist—perspectives of DuBois and Dewey. Our European heritage is racist. Our indigenous traditions are not.

PART I

Our Problem, Our Justice, Our Past

CHAPTER 2

Justice and Race

Abstract This chapter begins by describing a philosophy class discussion of a recently enacted Texas Voter Identification law. The class (mostly Republicans, but for one black female who is president of the local chapter of the National Association for the Advancement of Colored People (NAACP)) is divided by disagreement rooted in cultural difference, the same differences that divide American cultural and political worlds. The same cultural difference finds a home in confrontations between police and black men and boys; these confrontations I describe in some detail. Amadou Diallo appears, as do also Michael Brown and Darren Wilson, along with other instances of police shootings/killings of black men and boys. Justice questions get precise focus in all these situations of conflict. Western traditions of thought about justice find their way into virtually all our conversations about these particular situations that evoke judgments of justice and injustice.

Keywords Justice · Race · Michael Brown · Darren Wilson · Amadou Diallo · Principle · King Solomon

Our setting is an introductory philosophy class at Baylor University, a Baptist university in Waco, Texas. The Texas legislature has just passed a restrictive voter identification law. The class is filled with Republicans, or at least with students whose parents are Republicans. One exception is a black female who is president of the campus chapter

© The Author(s) 2018
S. Rosenbaum, *Race, Justice and American Intellectual Traditions*,
https://doi.org/10.1007/978-3-319-76198-5_2

of the National Association for the Advancement of Colored People (NAACP); she is the only black student in the class. The class has focused on issues related to classical sources in social and political philosophy.

The students are almost unanimous in support of the Texas legislature's action that strictly requires voter ID. A vocal exception is the female president of the campus chapter of the NAACP. What strikes the professor is a specific kind of obtuseness—a sort of blindness—in all of the students in the discussion.

The white Republican supporters of the voter ID law are blind to the constraints under which many poor Americans, especially poor black Americans, live. As natural to them as being college students is the idea of having a photo ID for voter identification. If they drive a car they must have a photo ID, and as Baylor students they have photo IDs. And voting is part of being a *citizen* of the United States. Requiring identification *as a citizen* to justify voting looks equally appropriate. Why would one *not* require a voter identification card?

What this group of students misses is historical context and the occasionally great hardship that makes it difficult for poor Americans, especially poor black Americans, to get to state offices where they might, with proper identification in hand, obtain the requisite voter ID. (One estimate put the number of Texas citizens deprived of voting rights by the voter ID requirement at 600,000. The exact number doesn't matter; suppose there are only 100, or even fewer.) The reason for students' failure to understand the human and political costs of the voter ID legislation is their cloistered cultural lives.

Such students have lived among peer groups of significant uniformity. Most had cars; most had spending money; most worried about their appearance and clothing; most had similar religious backgrounds; and the moral and social expectations resulting from those backgrounds were rather uniform. Also, those students had little appreciation of the American history that brings an intense focus to the issue of voter identification. They may have heard of, but they little appreciated, the significance of "Jim Crow" and "poll taxes." None of those historical injustices were part of their lives.

Those students suffered from a kind of ethnocentricity. Even in a university that sought cultural diversity, these students' exposure even to mildly different cultural contexts was limited. They were thus unable to appreciate the moral, social and political costs of a substantial voter ID requirement. And what about the black, female president of the campus NAACP chapter? Did she too suffer from a kind of ethnocentrism?

Not the same kind. Any president of any NAACP chapter is aware of and sensitive to the racial difference in American culture. This young woman was patient yet assertive in explaining her objections to the recently enacted Texas voter ID law, though her efforts were largely unsuccessful. Her objections got little sympathy because they were largely incomprehensible to her white Republican peers. The white students could little understand her claims about the accessibility of state offices where IDs might be gotten; and they could little understand her points about the difficulty of getting those personal documents—birth certificates, for example—legally required to get a Texas voter ID. Her difficulty lay in *not* understanding how the cultural realities of black life in Texas might elude bright, first-year college students of any race or gender. Those realities were obvious to her. The cultural cloister her white peers had grown up in was beyond her.

Cultural differences among these first-year college students account for their opinion differences. Families, churches, schools and general living circumstances systematically affect character, personality and opinion. Ethnocentrism is a common condition in the human world. Different kinds of cultural blindness pervade the human world. This introductory class of philosophy students exhibits one kind of cultural blindness. What we find in the following pages is that the ethnocentrism evident in this philosophy class is everywhere in our American world. We also find that even the most sophisticated intellectuals fall prey to the same ethnocentrism evident in this introductory philosophy class.

Regularity of experience breeds regularity of opinion and expectation; religion, morality and belief are wards of life experience, and those wards resist opposition or change. We humans are creative and resourceful in finding ways to resist change. We find many defenses against change of opinion or habit. The inertia bred into us by the regularity of experience resists change and finds many defenses against it. (Rational argument and adherence to guiding principles are some of those defenses.) Of special interest here, however, are different uses of common moral ideas we generally believe to be universal and common to all of us. Primary among those ideas is *justice*.

EXAMPLES

Racial difference has fomented discord of many kinds throughout American history. A dark continuity of discord between white and black Americans yields typical attitudes in almost every American. A vague result expresses itself in almost every American character, yielding habits of expectation, behavior and morality.

In encounters with different others, each of us responds in characteristic ways, depending on our backgrounds and previous contexts of interaction with different others.

Amadou Diallo

In 1999, Amadou Diallo died at the hands of four New York City policemen. Diallo was black; it was late night or early morning in a crime-ridden part of the city. The police ordered him to stop and show his hands. Diallo ran up his apartment steps—the porch light was out—reached for his wallet and was killed by 19 bullets—out of 42 fired—that found their mark. Diallo was a recent immigrant from Guinea, West Africa and had no weapon. Presumably, Diallo was reaching for his identification card. And presumably, the policemen mistakenly judged his reaching as aggressive and dangerous.

To imagine being in such a situation, *as* Diallo or *as* one of the policemen, is difficult for most of us; for the most part, our lives are routine and do not offer similar dangers for assessment and decision. But the circumstances of Diallo's death as we know them invite judgment.

Diallo was unarmed; he was out late night/early morning in a heavily patrolled part of the city. What was he doing? What would you or I be doing in similar circumstances? What would you or I think or do if four men we did not know to be police officers accosted us in such a place? Would we be afraid? Would we run away, run home? Putting to ourselves these questions stoke our imaginations and make difficult our "blaming" Diallo for what he did.

And the four policemen: Their job was to be suspicious, always suspicious, of anything or anybody out of the ordinary. A wandering black man at that time of the night/morning invited investigation. Suspicion creates suspects. Suspects must be investigated. Danger attends investigation of suspects. One must be ready for anything. One's life is in danger. But one has a duty, a job to do. And suspects in such circumstances are black. Black/white becomes, in that context, bad/good, as it becomes also dangerous/innocent. Those associations are integral to most parts of American culture. *Are those associations racism?*

Was Diallo a victim of racist police officers? Was he targeted *unjustly* because of his race? Was he killed *unjustly* because of his race?

One black man, unarmed. Four white police officers, each fully armed. Nobody to witness the killing. Nobody to *see* the racist behavior. Only the memory and words of the policemen. The circumstances invite a judgment of racism.

Diallo's family sued the city for $61 million and settled for $3 million. However one thinks about the issue of racism, one understands the power of that issue, not just its legal power but its moral power as well.

Since 1999 and Diallo's death, myriad similar situations have invited judgments of racism. Actions of police and frequently killings usually by white policemen of black men, have made large numbers of Americans uneasy about their culture. In addition to Diallo have been many others, too many to list, that since have provoked similar thoughts about racism.

AND OTHERS

Tamir Rice, the 12-year-old boy shot and killed in Cleveland by two white policemen on November 22, 2015; Mike Brown in Ferguson, Missouri, August 9, 2015; Walter Scott in Charleston, South Carolina on April 4, 2015; Philando Castille in Falcon Heights, Minnesota on July 6, 2016 and Jordan Edwards on May 2, 2017 in Mesquite, Texas. These are only a few killings of black men and boys by white policemen. Do these killings add up to racism, or even murder?

Testimony that the policemen involved are good people, responsible family members and good fathers is easy to get. These policemen are church members, soccer coaches, little league coaches and generally good people. Their jobs, however, put unusual pressures on them, and like all of us, they have habits, expectations and beliefs that make for their characters and behaviors. How might we know, or how might we judge that they are racists?

The significant evidence that such public servants are racists is the ongoing abuse and death at their hands of innocent black men. And sometimes women: July 10, 2015, Sandra Bland was stopped by police officer Brian Encinia in Waller County, Texas, for failing to signal her lane change. The encounter escalated and Bland was arrested; three days later she died in her jail cell, an apparent suicide by hanging.

The moral questions these cases raise are fundamental. How one answers such questions signifies not only how one thinks—and whether one thinks well or badly according to some standard—but also who one is as one has come to maturity in the various contexts that mingle to shape our characters.

QUESTIONS

In each of these cases, we must ask (1) What was going on in the minds of those involved? (2) Were they sufficiently sensitive to the others involved? (3) Were legal rights properly respected? and (4) Were customary moral expectations properly respected? These questions are of two kinds.

The first two questions concern character and personality. These questions are psychological and must be answered on a case-by-case basis. Humans are individuals having different genetic constitutions and different cultural and familial histories. Who I am and who you are—these are issues of our individuality, of how we *see* our situations, our possibilities and our worlds. Psychologists and social scientists seek generalizations that might illuminate individual behavior and suggest ways of understanding and improving it; however, the radical individuality that pulses in each of us is defiant and resists generalizations no matter how readily we may submit to studies and experiments; the task of social scientists is uniquely difficult. Fortunately, these scientific questions are not at issue here. This book is about *justice*. (Not that justice questions are *easier*!)

JUSTICE QUESTIONS

The second two questions are questions about justice. Properly respecting the rights of others is behaving justly; not doing so is behaving unjustly. Toward the situations of those mentioned above, one has a moral response, a feeling that somehow one person—in these situations usually the policeman involved—is not properly respecting the others morally or legally. This feeling, almost visceral, leads to claims of injustice. And recall too that, as in the philosophy class mentioned earlier, some kind of ethnocentrism is operating in all these situations.

When Michael Brown was shot to death in Ferguson, his friends and family and community—mostly black people—wanted justice; they thought his moral rights had not been respected. And Darren Wilson, the officer who shot the unarmed Brown multiple times, had similar support from largely white suburban communities nearby; in demonstrations in those white communities, support for Wilson again rested on claims of justice. The big problem in these situations is that their thought about justice moves different communities toward conflicting moral judgments. The black community supported Brown. The white community supported Wilson. At the base of both communities' thought was the idea of justice. The question cannot be avoided: What is justice, and how might our American world achieve it? And most importantly, *how might disagreements about justice be resolved?*

RACE, POVERTY, PRIVILEGE AND POLITICS

In all the cases mentioned, the ideas of race, poverty, privilege and politics are tangled into the mix. The white Republican students in a Republican state do not understand poverty *or* race, and they do not understand their own privilege. Those same students do not understand what poverty does to character and personality. And those same students are naïve about politics, its goals and its means. Such students are privileged. And so too are the police officers who killed Amadou Diallo, along with the officers in those other cases.

Those officers, like most, are well intentioned and trying to do their job. Like those first-year Republican students, the officers have contexts of life, habit, belief and expectation. For the officers, consequences of their character and their efforts to do their jobs sometimes produce abuses or deaths among the black people they are supposed to *serve*. The moral problem evident in all of these contexts, from classroom discussions to traffic stops and arrests, is the problem of justice—what it is and how to effect it.

Is the Texas voter ID law *unjust* in imposing strict constraints on who may vote? Is that law a new resonance with the long abandoned and *unjust* poll taxes now echoing in Republican controlled state legislatures? Did the four officers who killed Amadou Diallo do so *unjustly*? Did Michael Brown suffer *injustice* in his encounter with Darren Wilson? These questions of justice, of basic morality, are always right behind the raw feelings that boil up in response to many circumstances of living among different others. And these questions about the moral context of such situations cannot be avoided. How may we answer those questions?

BIBLICAL ANSWERS

These philosophical questions about justice find their way into every human culture, and they find different answers in different contexts. The Hebrew Bible/Old Testament offers answers coherent with primitive, nomadic conditions of life typical in Hebrew communities three or four millennia ago. Islamic cultures are rooted in that same Hebrew history and differ little from ancient Hebrew traditions' understandings of justice. In those traditions, justice is little different from goodness or uprightness of character. In both traditions, the character of the wise man as a source of justice is strong. King Solomon is a good example for those traditions of the wise practitioner of justice. Justice is a matter of character and exhibits itself as a particular response to a particular problem situation.

The well-known story of the two women each claiming a child as her own exhibits the wisdom and justice of Solomon. Each of the two women claimed the same child, since one of their two children had been stillborn during the same night. The women argued over the child, one claiming that the living child had been taken from her while she slept and the dead child left in its place. Solomon's response was to propose hacking the living child in half and giving half to each woman. As Solomon saw, the true mother was willing to give up her child in order to save its life. And the appropriateness of Solomon's judgment in that specific situation derives not from adherence to any general principles of justice but to wise judgment rooted in Solomon's own character. The particularity of these religious traditions' thought about justice, and their dependence on individual, charismatic individuals differs from Western, philosophical traditions of thought about justice.

WESTERN TRADITIONS OF JUSTICE

Western philosophical traditions about justice, unlike those religious traditions, take a distinctively *principled* approach to justice. Justice becomes a matter of discovering true principles rooted in the very idea of justice and then applying those principles in particular cases to get correct results. Having an intellectual understanding of justice *itself* enables knowing how to apply it in particular cases. This principled, intellectual approach to justice characterizes all Western, philosophical thought about it. Justice in this tradition is universal and knowable. The only alternative to its universality in Western thought about justice is that justice is "relative," dependent on context and conditions, and thus different in different times and places. Moral relativism is not tenable in the Western intellectual world.

In this characteristically Western philosophical approach, claims of justice and injustice require *intellectual* defense. Relevant arguments must be accessible to all, since everybody, we believe, has the same intellectual access to the same universal moral truths. Moral relativism, again, is untenable.

Since relativism is untenable in the Western world, moral views tend to come in distinct and opposing, and absolutist, forms. Consequentialist, deontological, divine command or virtue varieties of theory are dominant, and their proponents defend them cleverly and astutely. Since morality must be universal, and the only alternative to one or another form of universalism is relativism, some version of universalism *must* be true. (For an example of the rigor and comprehensiveness with which this philosophical task is engaged, see the defense of utilitarianism in the recent two-volume work, *On What Matters*, by Derek Parfit.) This tendency to think in an absolutist way about justice and morality is an integral part of Western intellectual culture in general, not just Western philosophy.

When Martin Luther King gave his "I Have a Dream" speech on the Washington mall in 1963, he believed he was speaking about the universal content of justice and morality, and likewise when he wrote his "Letter from a Birmingham Jail." And Michael Brown's friends and relatives, in asking for justice, believed they were asking for a simple requirement of universal morality. As did too the white demonstrators in defense of Darren Wilson. The absoluteness of justice and right, their universality, is integral to American thought about them. What one *sees* to be unjust—or just—*must* be unjust—or just, *given the proper understanding of justice.*

Although this general presumption of absolutism about morality and justice is pervasive in the American world—and indeed in the entire intellectual world of the West—we somehow cannot reach agreement about it in particular cases. Darren Wilson was not indicted by the Grand Jury in Ferguson, and their failure to indict him, in the view of Brown's fellow black citizens, was evidence of continuing racism in Ferguson and in the country in general. Those black citizens could *see* the racism in Brown's killing and in the Grand Jury's refusal to indict Wilson. The failure of others to see what they saw as plain as day could be only racist bigotry.

A CONUNDRUM

Notice a serious problem with this traditional Western Way of thinking about justice. If one *sees* what justice requires in a particular situation—and one sees well according to universal, impartial standards or principles of justice itself—then *what can be wrong with those who simply do not see what one sees so clearly?* What obscures their vision? What interferes with their understanding of this basic moral idea?

Perhaps some intellectual or moral defect in their character disables them? Indeed what else might disable them other than intellectual or moral defect embedded in their character? And perhaps such defect is unknown to them, or not accessible by them?

If one believes, in a way completely typical of Westerners, that basic moral truths are in principle accessible by all and by relatively straightforward, perhaps intellectual, technique, then how may we account for basic moral disagreements among earnest Americans? Simple reasoning *must* yield agreement apart from some obstruction or defect, moral or intellectual.

The obstruction or defect we typically think impedes others' judgment is prejudice or bigotry. Only such intellectual/moral defect might explain the obtuseness of those who simply cannot see what we see so clearly and know to be true. Where differences about a police shooting—is it just or unjust—become prominent, our only recourse is to *explain the obtuseness of those who disagree with us* by their racism, their bigotry and prejudice.

In sum, our embrace of universal absolutism about basic morality means we have no recourse other than to explain the disagreement of others by reference to their character defect, by their racism, bigotry or prejudice. We *must* see intellectual or moral defect in those who disagree with us about justice.

In the Michael Brown case, when the Grand Jury did not indict Darren Wilson, our only recourse was to see that jury as racist. How otherwise could they deliver a judgment so obviously mistaken? And for the white suburban demonstrators supporting Darren Wilson, our only recourse was to see them as likewise racists. Racism obscures moral judgment; it clouds moral vision. When others do not see what we see so clearly, they must have "vision problems"; they must be racists.

Our Western culture of moral absolutism requires us to explain the obtuseness of others by their defect of intellectual or moral character. Nothing else can explain their failure to see what is so obvious to us.

This conundrum will be with us throughout this book; it is important because it limits our ability to deal effectively with moral disagreement. Where others are obtuse or ill-informed or thoughtless or bigoted, we have no recourse for dealing with them other than by somehow "getting them out of the way." Our effort to get them out of the way in our American world is frequently by legal means, as it is in most Western democracies; we do not resort to "vigilante justice" or to killing them, as happens in many other parts of the world. We may hope that in our democratic world we need not "write people off" because of defects in their moral or intellectual character, but how may we realize that hope?

Being a community, a community that can come to a basic agreement about moral issues of justice, requires us to see these moral conflicts differently. Showing how to see such basic conflicts differently is the primary task of this book. Indeed, the central issue this book addresses is how we might think about justice in a way that does not exclude differently thinking others from our own moral community. Justice must become an *inclusive* idea, one that does not seek or mandate conquest of differently thinking others.

We need not see others who disagree with us about moral basics as obtuse or as prejudiced or as racists. In fact, *not* seeing those who disagree with us as benighted or bigoted is fundamental to progress toward agreement about morally basic ideas like justice.

Our next task is to review the most prominent Western philosophical theories of justice and morality, those that definitively shape our resources for dealing with issues of morality that significantly divide us. Only by understanding where our attitudes have originated, and how they have perpetuated themselves, may we find more constructive roots for a different way of engaging these questions. This chapter explains the most prominent source of Western traditions of thought about justice and morality, Plato.

CHAPTER 3

Western Justice

Abstract I begin with a brief account of Platonism and explain how it lives in current Western, especially American, culture. Plato's thought infuses our respect for authorities, even though our authorities are not (as Plato would prefer) an intellectual elite. I return to the Michael Brown/Darren Wilson confrontation and try to find some analogue of the respect for authority that pervades our culture in their confrontation. I then give a brief account of *The Republic* to see how its search for justice yields something similar to, though different from, our own understanding of justice. Our difference from Plato appears, for example, in our respect for characters regardless of their intellectual ability; Forrest Gump is the prominent example here. The chapter concludes by raising questions about Plato's account of justice in the context of our current needs for justice in racially freighted confrontations like that between Michael Brown and Darren Wilson.

Keywords Platonism · *The Republic* · Forrest Gump · Authority

Western thought about justice, indeed about all morality, comes mainly out of the ancient Greek world, especially out of Plato. Plato sets the basic foundations and parameters for Western thought about morality, and seldom has Western thought deviated far from its distinctive Platonist foundation.

PLATO'S VALUE WORLD

In Plato's world, understanding the *intellectual content* of any idea is required for successful functioning with that idea. Each of Plato's dialogues illustrates this primacy of intellectual understanding for any basic idea. If one wants to be courageous, then one must know what courage *is in itself*; one must understand its intellectual content in order to *be* courageous. (See Plato's *Laches*.)

In *Euthyphro*, Socrates insists that Euthyphro's effort to do what is pious or holy requires understanding what piety or holiness *is*. The intellectual task is prerequisite to *being* righteous or holy or *doing* what is righteous or holy. In Plato's world, grasping the intellectual content of any idea is the condition of using that idea successfully.

In *Theatetus*, one must understand what knowledge is in order to have knowledge; knowing requires understanding the intellectual content of the *idea* of knowledge. And so it goes in each of Plato's well-known dialogues. The theme that knowledge of its intellectual content necessarily precedes successful use of any idea is a defining characteristic of Platonism. In the Western world, this Platonist idea is foundational to thought about issues of value.

(For these dialogues, and more, see *Plato: Complete Works*, 1997.)

Exceptions to this Platonism and its absolutism about value appear occasionally in our Western world. Nietzsche, for example, mocked Plato's presumption about the powers of our intellect; Nietzsche saw humans as simply animals, indeed as "irrational" animals incapable of the intellectual feats Plato required. (Indeed a notable characteristic of each of Plato's dialogues is its *failure* to get the desired account of intellectual content the dialogue aims at, a fact that at least coheres with Nietzsche's skepticism.) In any case, Nietzsche fell from his self-appointed position as critic of Western Platonism because of his vulnerability to the charge of relativism.

RELATIVISM

If one denies there is an absolute answer to questions about value, then one has, in Plato's view, no way to get beyond differing opinions about value. If one denies that righteousness is of a single, knowable nature, then one must fall back on different and frequently irreconcilable opinions about it.

Does righteousness require killing apostates? Does it require shunning gay or lesbian couples? Does it require giving 10% of one's income to the Church? Does it require voting for antiabortion political candidates? Answers to these questions are different for almost anybody who considers them. Are all of these people *right* in their differing opinions about such issues? Not all of these conflicting opinions can be right. There must be a single, correct answer rooted in the very idea of righteousness; otherwise, "anything goes!" Nietzsche's scorn of Plato's respect for human intellectual ability fails in the face of his apparent relativism, his apparent belief that, where values are concerned, "anything goes." And if "anything goes," then power alone is one's only recourse. (And this recourse makes Hitler appear a natural political outcome of Nietzsche's thought.)

The bottom line for our Platonism in the Western world is that we are instinctively absolutists. We cannot see beyond the absolutism Plato gave us. For any value question, there is one and only one *right* answer, and that answer is knowable by our intellects. One other feature of Plato's absolutism about value is important to our social thought about justice.

PLATONIST CERTAINTY

When one knows the content of any value idea, one simply *knows* it. If one has gone through the knowing process, then one has the result of that process, knowledge. When one has knowledge, then one properly relies on that knowledge. In Plato's intellectual world knowing what justice is or what rightness is or what holiness is gives one the power to *use* that knowledge, to act on it.

The issue of abortion provides a succinct example. To know that abortion is wrong is to have authorization for actions against abortion. To know that abortion is not wrong is to have authorization for performing abortions.

In Plato's Western world, to know something is to have the power to act; knowledge yields power. When one is right, when one knows, then one must behave according to what one knows. If others disagree, they are wrong—and one knows they are wrong because their opinion differs from one's own; they have made a mistake.

Plato Summary

Plato gives us two views about values that have become "second nature" in Western thought about value; the views are so deeply embedded in our thinking that we cannot think otherwise about value.

1. Our values are absolute and knowledge of them results from intellectual inquiry—"dialectic" is Plato's normal term for such inquiry. We ask and answer; we propose "theories" and we give "counterexamples." (Plato's *Euthyphro* is a straightforward example of the technique.) The end result of this dialectical process is (ideally) that we arrive at the correct answer to our question. (That none of Plato's dialogues achieves this ideal of arriving at the correct answer did not deter Plato nor does it deter us, his intellectual descendents.)
2. Our value beliefs are certain; they result from an appropriate inquiry that yields a result we can act on. The correctness of our value beliefs is integral to our Platonist heritage.

These two views are our principal heritage, our inheritance from more than two millennia of Western culture rooted in Platonism. These views appear whenever people use basic value ideas, ideas like justice, rightness, wrongness, injustice, good and bad.

In Plato's world, the correctness of any view derives from its roots in intellectual authority, the authority of acute, comprehensive thought that is able to achieve its goal of knowledge—knowledge about courage, about piety, about justice and about virtue. That intellectual authority is absolute, much as is the authority of "the sorting hat" in Harry Potter's world to discriminate which Hogwarts house an aspiring wizard must join.

The power of authority enables every human to see and do and be. Respect for that power is rooted, at least in the Western world, in the thought of Plato. In Plato, authority resides with the intellectually gifted, those who are able to engage in dialectic most effectively and thereby to achieve real knowledge.

Authorities

Plato's respect for human intellectual skill as the ultimate authority over human morality and society comes into the contemporary world with less vigor than it had in Plato's thought. In today's cultural world, intellectual ability on its own gets little recognition. We speak of "ivory tower academics" as intellectuals detached from "the real world" in which real people live real lives. We little trust academics, and we find them inevitably "liberal" by contrast with those of us who must make our ways "in the real world." We tolerate them largely because they are part of the established institutions that give us the credentials we need to make our way successfully in the real world. The bottom line for us contemporaries is that we have no respect for "eggheads" or ivory-tower refuges from the real world in which the rest of us must live. However, though unlike Plato we distrust intellectuals, various authorities do guide our behavior and control our values.

If we are Catholics, then customarily we defer to priest, bishop and Pope. If we are atheists—like Daniel Dennett or Ron Reagan—we defer (as Plato would prefer) to "rational argument." If we are fundamentalist Christians, we defer to the authoritative word of God—frequently as literally expressed in the seventeenth century King James translation of the Bible. Though we have turned away from Plato on the issue of what correct authority is—intellectual, dialectical skill just doesn't "do it" for us anymore—we nonetheless defer to one authority or another in coming to our value beliefs.

Is abortion wrong? We have the answer and we have our authority. Is marriage equality wrong? Again we have the answer and we have our authority. And so it is for virtually any other issue of value controversy we might confront. On the issue of race, however, our situation is different.

RACE, AUTHORITY AND JUSTICE

Michael Brown was part of a family and various communities that saw him as a deserving individual struggling with his own issues and needs, and trying to make his way into a constructive future. In Brown's confrontation with Darren Wilson, he was not among his own family and communities, and the results of that confrontation were unpredictable, since there was not a web of relationship that had specific expectations of the confrontation. Of course, Brown and Wilson might have "followed rules" that might have lessened the likelihood of a destructive result from their confrontation. But generally, one does not "follow rules" when interacting with others; one has typical patterns of behavior and expectation that, along with instincts and impulses yield one's behavior. And also, one is more or less "mature" in one's belief, behavior and action.

In the interaction between Brown and Wilson, each was thrown back on resources that were not involved in their customary family and community relationships. Were these resources or authorities constructively involved in their interaction? If not, what were their resources or authorities in that situation? Bible? Pope? Reason?

None of these traditional authorities was involved. Rather both Brown and Wilson saw themselves as somehow empowered to treat the other as each did; they saw themselves, as the individuals they were, properly controlling their own behavior. For Brown, the police were stereotypes, "enemies" who did not respect him; for Wilson too, Brown was a stereotype, an "enemy" who did not respect him. In such situations, one's resources are neither one's usual authorities for value issues, nor do they include—at least directly—one's family or communities.

"INTERNAL AUTHORITY"

Their authorities were not ideas of justice or right and wrong; rather their authority was their understanding of themselves *as the individuals they were* along with their need for recognition *as* who they were, perhaps "respect" from those they encountered. In this situation, relevant authorities are not *external* to either of them but are *internal* to each of them. And like others in such situations, they were "making up" their "game plan" at the very time they were "playing the game." The rules or principles that might come from "external authorities" were not present.

The "internal authority" that guided them, spontaneously and creatively, is nonetheless an authority, and it requires respect as much as do Pope, reason or Bible. The respect for authority that seems so obvious in the case of issues like abortion, marriage equality and freedom from religion persists in these cases as well, but it takes a different form. Consequently, the authorities that appear in the contemporary world as surrogates for the reason or intellect of Plato nonetheless derive from the same intellectual history that begins in the Western world with Plato. And those authorities, we consistently believe, invest us with the same confidence in our own rectitude that, in Plato's thought, comes from intellectual resources.

Plato remains the source of Western intellectual culture's commitment to authority as the solution to our value questions. The dislocation of contemporary American culture from Plato's ideals of reason and certainty is only modest; we remain Platonists in our thought about value issues. Authority and certainty are the roots of our thought about value. We must engage the question how to understand the *internal authorities* that guide us in situations that become confrontations; these situations require judgments of justice or injustice, and evaluations of behavior. Michael Brown and Darren Wilson, and their confrontation, invite our deliberation and judgment. But for the moment, consider what Plato explicitly tells us about justice.

THE REPUBLIC

The Republic is Plato's longest extant dialogue and is made up of twelve books. The frame for the entire work is the idea of justice: What is justice? In this way, the dialogue is completely typical; getting an intellectual account of the idea of justice is the goal of the dialogue. But that goal, explicitly similar to the goals of other dialogues, leads in *The Republic* to an unconventional strategy for getting at that content. Instead of the intellectual dialectic characteristic of other dialogues, in *The Republic* Socrates resorts to an analogy, the analogy between justice in the individual and justice in the state. The assumption is that justice in the state may be easier to see since it is "bigger," but also that seeing it in the state enables seeing it in the individual, even though the individual is "smaller" than the state. (Small letters are more difficult to read at a distance than are large letters!)

Most of the dialogue after Book 2 is devoted to justice "writ large" in the state. To make a long and interesting story very short, justice in the state is the harmony of all parts of the state under the guidance of the intellectual elite, those who *know*.

Plato's commitment to stratification of classes, genders and races under the guidance of the intellectual elite is absolute. Apart from the authority of those who *know* and are qualified to manage those who are less able, the state must decline into disorder. The authority of the guardians, the intellectual class, must be absolute as a condition of order and harmony in the state. American disdain for the intellectual elite provides a clue to the natural opinion of Americans about Plato's idea of justice.

We Americans do not respect the intellectual elite; we see them as ivory tower residents remote from real life and unable to deliver judgments about it. In so far as Plato does not respect individuals *as* individuals, we descendants of the Enlightenment cannot respect his view about justice. And in fact, Plato's view about justice does not help at all with the project of figuring out what justice requires in cases like Michael Brown's confrontation with Darren Wilson. Plato's idea of justice is all about order, order in the state and order in individual psyches. (In fairness, we should admit that in Plato's *Republic*, stratification among classes, genders and races would never yield the sort of confrontations between races that have become common in recent American culture. The structures put in place by Plato's intellectually elite ruling class would preclude such confrontations.)

As in the just state, the intellectual class must rule, so in individuals having the virtue of justice reason must rule. In so far as one is really smart and "rational," then one has a chance to be a just person. One must control, under the guidance of reason and intellect, one's emotions and appetites. Some individuals will be unable to control passion and appetite rationally; those individuals are "lost causes" where justice or virtue are concerned.

Notice again, the discord between Plato's commitment to rational order in individuals and the typical American commitment to respect for individuals *as* individuals, whether or not they are "rational."

FORREST GUMP

One hero of recent American culture is Forrest Gump. Forrest is the hero of the film bearing his name as title. Forrest's primary characteristic is his intellectual limitation; his IQ is 80. Forrest is not among any intellectual elite. Forrest is nevertheless as "good" as any individual one might encounter; he has "good common sense," and he is morally "as good as they come."

Forrest remembers his mother's wisdom, and it guides all his decisions and behavior. ("Stupid is as stupid does.") Forrest's wisdom is not the fruit of intellectual gifts. One might say that Forrest is an American counterexample to Plato's idea that justice, order or harmony is the fruit only of acute intellectual gifts. American deference to authority does not extend to those who are intellectually gifted.

Other American heroes are perhaps equally examples of our dissent from Plato's commitment to reason and intellect. John Wayne, perhaps Abraham Lincoln and other American heroes have their heroic stature not because of their intellectual gifts, but because of their wisdom, charisma or other individual quality. American respect for intellect and rationality is limited. Forrest Gump is probably the best exemplar of why American deference to Plato is limited. Our individualism shoulders aside Plato's respect for rational or intellectual authority.

CONCLUDING REMARKS ABOUT PLATO

Plato's respect for intellectual and rational authority pervades his dialogues. What remains of that respect in the contemporary Western world is respect for authority, although not the authority that derives from intellectual prowess. Plato's respect for authority remains.

And too, the conviction, the certainty, that Plato saw deriving from respect for proper authority does remain with us. Our certainties, however, derive from different authorities—God, Reason, the Bible, the Koran or other sacred text.

About these Platonist commitments of American (and more generally Western) culture many questions may, of course, be asked. Some questions are inevitable once the historical context comes into focus.

Why do we no longer respect rational or intellectual skill in the same way Plato did? Why do even our scientists get low marks for the results of their studies, studies that are specifically designed to be objective, dispassionate and conclusive? Why is Forrest Gump a more compelling model than, say, Daniel Dennett or Simon Blackburn, sophisticated philosophers who are atheists and naturalists? And why do we nonetheless believe our values are certain and are preferable to those of others? Why are our authorities more trustworthy than the authorities of those with whom we disagree? All these questions and many more come easily into focus when we become aware of our intellectual heritage.

A LAST QUESTION

When we consider practices, policies or behaviors about which we might form a conviction—abortion, marriage equality, gender reversal or others—we appeal to our favored authority—Pope, Reason or sacred text. However, when we consider freighted occasions of confrontation—like that between Michael Brown and Darren Wilson—we find those customary authorities are unavailable for forging or explaining our behaviors. In those confrontations, we must have recourse to what I called earlier the *internal authority* of our characters.

How does—or can—our spontaneity in such situations conform to the Platonism that otherwise insinuates itself into the value structures of Western culture? In such situations, no external authority controls our behavior; only the internal authority of our characters is available. Perhaps this extreme divergence from Platonism, where rational—or other—authority is always in control, means we must look to some other tradition to account for our recourse in such situations of confrontation? And notice also that in such situations the ideas of justice, rightness, goodness and badness are as applicable as they are in situations where our behaviors fall under some external authority.

We need an idea of justice that enables it in both of these situations—those where our behavior is controlled by an external authority and those where it is controlled by ourselves, by our internal authority. Such an idea of justice cannot be found within our Platonist intellectual traditions. We must look elsewhere; we must look beyond the Western intellectual heritage rooted in Plato. A viable alternative to our Platonist tradition about justice appears in Part II.

Our next task is to examine an influential Enlightenment perspective that perpetuates the Platonism we have just found deficient in enabling our understanding of justice—as well as other basic value ideas—in some of the most important situations we confront. Consider next the nineteenth-century perspective of John Stuart Mill.

CHAPTER 4

John Stuart Mill and the Liberal Tradition

Abstract This chapter begins with a brief account of how we get from Plato's idea of reason, through Aristotle and the scientific revolution of the seventeenth century, to a slightly different and Enlightenment-inspired idea of reason. Reason, during the Enlightenment, took on again the autonomy from culture that it had for Plato. Mill is the character who expresses most vigorously the individualism prominent in Western intellectual culture, especially in American culture. Mill's *On Liberty* is a definitive expression of the Enlightenment ideal of individual autonomy. Mill, unfortunately, turns out to be a thorough-going racist; his thought about India expresses that racism. Mill's attitude toward residents of India resembles the attitude of Paula Ramsey Taylor toward Michelle Obama and Ms. Obama's then-impending replacement by Melania Trump. ("It will be so refreshing to have a classy, beautiful, dignified First Lady back in the White House. I'm tired of seeing a (sic) Ape in heels.")

Keywords Aristotle · Enlightenment · John Stuart Mill · *On Liberty* India · British East India Company

The move from Plato to Mill leaps over more than two millennia of intellectual history. Mill is one of the most prominent moralists of the nineteenth century and is a product of the Western Enlightenment. The story of the Enlightenment is complex, intricate and subtle. My excuse for this grand leap is not a desire to avoid that story but rather the desire to focus on intellectual backgrounds for contemporary thought about justice. Here is a "quick and dirty" account of the journey from Plato to the nineteenth century. (Feel free to skip this section and go straight to Mill's thought in the next.)

ARISTOTLE

Plato's student Aristotle is much more "down to earth" than Plato. For Aristotle, moral character is a result of habituation by families and communities rather than reflective reasoning. Aristotle's divergence from Plato on this score makes Aristotle more congenial to "real world" accounts of virtue and justice; Aristotle's view accords with our natural instincts about virtue and justice; those things result from training and habituation. And in Aristotle's view about character, our natural instincts about people like Forrest Gump find a natural home; our instincts accord more easily with Aristotle's view about these matters than with Plato's. Though Aristotle brings thought about these issues "down to earth," he agrees with Plato to the extent of believing that the best life one might live is an intellectual life.

In Aristotle, thinkers—mathematicians, philosophers and theorists—are better than craftsmen, artists or merchants; their intellectual activities are superior to the practical activities that motivate craftsmen, artists and merchants. In this way, the intellectualism definitive of Platonism finds its way into Plato's student, Aristotle. In Ralph Waldo Emerson's memorable words, "A wise man will see that Aristotle Platonizes" ("Circles," *Emerson's Essays*, 1995).

Aristotle's deference to intellect is as thorough as is Plato's. But Aristotle's philosophical views are more comprehensive than Plato's. Aristotle is interested in the "factual" world as well as the "value" world, and he theorizes about virtually everything. Aristotle became known as "The Philosopher," and his theories dominated the intellectual world of the West until the Enlightenment; for almost two millennia Aristotle's theories consolidated their inertia in the Western world. The key to Aristotle's theorizing about the physical world—as about everything—is the idea of *teleology*.

Every part of the physical world has a point, a goal, a proper end, a *telos*. Every action of every creature has a goal, and the creature itself has a proper end, its *telos*. Aristotelian teleology encompasses all of science, even physics and cosmology.

Five basic elements make up Aristotle's "periodic table": earth, water, air, fire and ether. The essential properties of each element in Aristotle's table of elements are (1) its natural motion and (2) its proper place in an ideal sorting out of the elements in nature. Earth and water naturally move downward; they *want* to get where they belong. Air and fire naturally move upward; they too *want* to get where they belong. Ether naturally moves circularly about the center of the earth. (Since Ether is already where it wants to be, it's motion is serene since it has no desire to get anywhere.)

The impetus for Aristotle's teleological physics comes from its agreement with observation. Objects do behave roughly in the ways Aristotle's physics predicts. Teleology is the key to Aristotle's physics and to his understanding of reality in general. All explanation, all theory, *just is* teleological.

The authority of Aristotle—united in the twelfth century with the authority of The Church by St. Thomas Aquinas—dominated Western culture for almost two millennia. Aristotle's teleology meshed well with orthodox Christian doctrine, and the unity of the entire intellectual world yielded a comfortable inertia to all of life under the guidance of Church authority.

ENLIGHTENMENT SCIENCE

The Enlightenment, beginning around the turn of the seventeenth century, destroyed this comfortable inertia. Galileo was a central figure in the downfall of Aristotelian, teleological physics. Galileo, along with Thomas Hobbes and other unconventional thinkers, enabled the idea that the physical world was material and mechanical, and that events were controlled, not by teleological "laws," but by impersonal laws of motion. Matter in motion, and the mechanical laws that govern it provided the new, Enlightenment vision of science. The course of the seventeenth century is the story of the ongoing displacement of Aristotelian teleology; that displacement culminates in Isaac Newton's 1687 *Principia Mathematica*. In the intellectual culture of the late seventeenth and early eighteenth centuries, Newton was a genius. In Alexander Pope's famous couplet that became Newton's epitaph,

Nature and nature's laws lay hid in night.
God said, Let Newton be! And all was light!

Newton's laws of motion displaced Aristotelian teleological physics. Newton's laws were mechanical and did not tolerate teleology. Newton gave strong impetus to our contemporary—and still Enlightenment—understanding of science, along with its orientation toward searching for regularities explained by mechanical, impersonal law. With Newton's success, science transformed into the material, mechanical enterprise of contemporary science.

The Return of Reason

The unity of the worlds of science, religion, morality and society under the guidance of Aristotelian—and Thomistic—teleology disappeared during the seventeenth century. Newtonian physics tore the intellectual world of science away from the unified authority located then primarily in The Church. The "new," ascendant authority opposing Church authority was, once again, *reason*. During the Enlightenment, however, that authoritative reason was no longer independent, as it was in Plato, of experience. Science was the ascendency of reason *and* experience, united in their opposition to the authority of The Church. Proper authority in matters philosophical, scientific and moral was, once again, reason itself. (The history of seventeenth- and eighteenth-century philosophy is a record of the struggle to recapture, to any extent possible, some coherence between the claims of The Church in matters religious, moral and social and the claims of reason, then powerfully ascendant under the impetus of Newtonian physics.)

No longer was religious authority proper guidance for those parts of life now external to The Church. Reason again, and reason alone, must provide whatever guidance is possible for knowledge of nature, society and morality. (The authority of The Church incurred further damage even to its religious authority from the Protestant Reformation beginning in the sixteenth century.) Those Enlightenment times were especially harrowing for The Church and its emissaries.

The separation of morality from the authority of The Church inspired significant creativity among philosophers in their search to bring morality once again under the authority of reason alone. John Stuart Mill was among the leading moralists of the nineteenth century who sought to realize that goal of a world no longer subject to Church authority. Mill had enormous influence on subsequent moral and social thinkers. (The larger story of Enlightenment moral theory is too complex to tell here, though it is very interesting for those of a philosophical turn of mind.)

JOHN STUART MILL (1806–1873)

John Stuart Mill is both a utilitarian and a libertarian. Mill's essay *On Liberty* (1859) advocates classical liberalism; indeed, that essay *defines* classical liberalism and produces strong conviction in many who read it. *On Liberty* tells us what individual freedom *is* and *must be* in contexts where political power might seek to subordinate it. The following words from *On Liberty* are among the most famous in all of philosophy:

> The object of this Essay is to assert one very simple principle, as entitled to govern absolutely the dealings of society with the individual in the way of compulsion and control, whether the means used be physical force in the form of legal penalties or the moral coercion of public opinion. That principle is, that the sole end for which mankind are warranted, individually or collectively, in interfering with the liberty of action of any of their number, is self-protection. That the only purpose for which power can be rightfully exercised over any member of a civilized community, against his will, is to prevent harm to others. His own good, either physical or moral, is not a sufficient warrant. He cannot rightfully be compelled to do or forbear because it will be better for him to do so, because it will make him happier, because, in the opinions of others, to do so would be wise, or even right. These are good reasons for remonstrating with him, or reasoning with him, or persuading him, or entreating him, but not for compelling him, or visiting him with any evil in case he do otherwise. To justify that, the conduct from which it is desired to deter him, must be calculated to produce evil to some one else. The only part of the conduct of any one, for which he is amenable to society, is that which concerns others. In the part which merely concerns himself, his independence is, of right, absolute. Over himself, over his own body and mind, the individual is sovereign. (*On Liberty*, 2003)

As Mill notes, his intent is to *assert* the "very simple principle," not to argue for it as a universal truth. Mill does make a significant case for the principle; he does in fact "argue" for it especially as regards freedom of speech and expression. Mill does not, however, make an argument for the *absoluteness* of the principle as he asserts it in the quotation.

Indeed, Mill does not believe this principle applies universally to all humanity; as he puts it, the principle applies only to "any member of a civilized community," but not to "barbarians." During the thirty-five years preceding Mill's writing of this essay, he was working for the British East India Company, and he did believe that native Indian humans were *not* members of civilized communities, and that his very simple principle did not apply to them. The Indian subcontinent was properly under British control, and its native inhabitants were properly subjects of Britain, since they were not civilized peoples.

In Mill's account of British colonies, he makes clear his understanding of natives of those colonies as not civilized peoples. The colonies are

> hardly to be looked upon as countries ... but more properly as outlying agricultural or manufacturing estates belonging to a larger community. Our West Indian colonies, for example, cannot be regarded as countries with a productive capital of their own ... [but are rather] the place where England finds it convenient to carry on the production of sugar, coffee and a few other tropical commodities. (Quoted in Curtin, Deane, *Chinnagounder's Challenge*, 1999, 36)

And Mill's teacher Jeremy Bentham makes an example of Indian behavior as uncivilized.

> An Indian receives an injury, real or imaginary, from an Indian of another tribe. He revenges it upon the person of his antagonist with the most excruciating torments: the case being, that cruelties inflicted on such an occasion, gain him reputation in his own tribe. The disposition manifested in such a case can never be deemed a good one, among a people ever so few degrees advanced, in point of civilization, above the Indians. (Bentham, Jeremy, *Collected Works*, 1995, 130)

A general tendency among sophisticated British thinkers of Mill's generation was to see natives of colonized lands as uncivilized and undeserving of the rights and privileges of civilized peoples.

Mill's liberalism, his assertion of the rights of people in civilized society to freedom from coercion and control by political authorities—and limited to civilized peoples—has come powerfully into the American world where it animates one of our distinctive political perspectives. An example of that political perspective appears in the contemporary American world in the political life of Paul Ryan, Speaker of the House of Representatives in 2017. Ryan's political perspective has more recent, American roots also, including Ayn Rand and Milton Friedman, but Mill is the most prominent classical, Enlightenment source of that perspective.

Mill's reservations about natives of the Indian subcontinent were that they were not civilized people and needed guidance from imperial powers that were able to judge what policies, practices and behaviors were appropriate for them. Barbarians—along with children and mentally challenged individuals even in civilized countries—needed control; they were incapable of the judgment that comes only with civilization.

Mill was one of the brightest and best of nineteenth-century intellectuals. Mill was as enlightened as any man of his time, one who favored even allowing women the right to vote. Sexist Mill was not. Was Mill Racist?

How otherwise might one explain Mill's defense of British imperialism? How otherwise might one explain Mill's conclusion that native residents of the Indian subcontinent needed British, authoritarian control?

One of Western civilization's best, brightest and most enlightened nineteenth-century thinkers appears to have remained in the clutches of a primal bigotry. Hard conclusion to swallow. But if we can choke that conclusion down, perhaps we may become able to understand phenomena in our contemporary world that otherwise elude us.

The shooting of Michael Brown by Darren Wilson in Ferguson, Missouri brought, along with calls for justice, many responses likely also rooted in a primal bigotry. The demonstrations in Ferguson itself by the black community elicited large military-style responses from the largely white Ferguson police department. These confrontation-style interactions with massive force arrayed on the side of the police were breaches of civility. What explains these breaches of civility?

Like Mill's conviction that the barbarians of the Indian subcontinent needed British control, the police of Ferguson held—and acted on—the conviction that the black community of Ferguson needed police control. The presumption on both sides—in nineteenth-century Britain and in 2014 America—was that barbarians need authoritarian control. This conclusion may seem harsh. Mill's blindness of almost 150 years ago surely does not linger still in the contemporary American world?

Most certainly that blindness lingers still. In the contemporary American world, that blindness appears as "racism." The black community in Ferguson believes they are treated unjustly, that the white police are racists. The white police, under the rhetorical guise of "law and order" and "keeping the peace," deny they are racists. Are the police in Ferguson racists? Consider another, perhaps less freighted situation that leads to the same question.

After the Presidential election of 2016, the Mayor of Clay, West Virginia, Pamela Ramsey Taylor posted on Facebook her response to Donald Trump having won that election:

It will be so refreshing to have a classy, beautiful, dignified First Lady back in the White House. I'm tired of seeing a (sic) Ape in heels.

What Ms. Taylor said about Mrs. Obama was not politically correct, but it did reveal something—but what? Ms. Taylor's racism? Here is what Ms. Taylor said in response to the accusation of racism:

> My comment was not intended to be racist at all. I was referring to my day being made for change in the White House! I am truly sorry for any hard feeling this may have caused! Those who know me know that I'm not of any way racist! Again, I would like to apologize for this getting out of hand!

In our contemporary world, the public character of social media makes difficult being always politically correct; that means in this case that concealing one's true attitudes—as political correctness presumably requires—is more difficult.

Ms. Taylor's remark "was not intended" to be racist; that is, she did not intentionally speak her racism. Ms. Taylor was "truly sorry for any hard feeling" her remark might have caused. Ms. Taylor apologized for "this getting out of hand!" What Ms. Taylor did not do is apologize for *her remark*. Ms. Taylor's racism drips from her original posting.

Ms. Taylor's racism is evident in her posting even if not (retrospectively) to herself. To Ms. Taylor, her inspection of her own psyche reveals that she is not a racist, as she believes is evident to anybody who knows her. And presumably, no more than her racism was evident to Ms. Taylor was John Stuart Mill's imperialist, authoritarian racism evident to him. The testimony of Mill's blind spot about his own racism is replicated again and again in the contemporary American world.

We Americans embrace Enlightenment moral and social values, yet because of our own American history we too have "blind spots" that conceal from us the content of our own psyches. Mill believed only "civilized" individuals were entitled to individual autonomy, thus excluding the barbarians of the Indian subcontinent. Ms. Taylor believed an ape in heels was not a proper first lady. Ms. Taylor's ignorance of the content of her own psyche is not uncommon in the American world. Our psyches are not transparent—not to others *and not to ourselves*. Our psyches do, however, occasionally reveal themselves in posts on social media.

Given the opacity of our psyches to ourselves as well as to others, what should we make of the ubiquitous talk about justice in our moral and social worlds? We speak as though we know what justice looks like and how to achieve it, though in a world in which we do not know ourselves how can we "see" either justice or how we might achieve it?

MILL'S LIBERALISM AGAIN

Mill's moral values, his liberal individualism and his respect for individual autonomy are prominent in the contemporary American world. Paul Ryan, along with Rand Paul, and a raft of additional conservative Republicans embrace and defend those values. Governmental imposition on individuals should not, according to these thinkers, be encouraged or tolerated. Individual freedom is the great goal of the Enlightenment and is realized most fully in the American world. These politicians believe that every effort must be made to preserve and encourage that freedom. The moral, social and political implications of this Enlightenment perspective remain strong in our American world. Precisely what those implications are becomes clear in the next chapter on Milton Friedman. For now, however, think again about the question posed above about Mill's primal bigotry and its continuance in the contemporary American world.

Does such primal bigotry *impede* the Enlightenment respect for individual freedom? Given the examples considered above, the only possible conclusion is that it does. How otherwise might we explain or understand Mill's failure to see native residents of the Indian subcontinent as deserving of the same freedom and autonomy as "civilized" citizens of the British Empire? This most enlightened of British citizens failed to see native Indians as deserving of freedom. Can there be another explanation than Mill's own primal bigotry? (For a film expression of the same bigotry that infected Mill, see the PBS television series, "Indian Summers.")

One might try to explain Mill's distinction between residents of civilized communities and barbarians by a need to profit from exploiting the natural resources of India. This strategy, however, makes of Mill—one of the most enlightened of British citizens—a perfect hypocrite. Probably Mill's cultural or psychological blindness is a better recourse for explaining his perspective than making of him a calculating hypocrite. And surely the same is true of those contemporary American examples of a similar blindness mentioned above.

Pamela Ramsey Taylor did not see her own racism any more than John Stuart Mill saw his. Ms. Taylor likely believed firmly in the values of individual freedom and autonomy, but *for whom?* Surely not "a ape in heels."

Apes are no better morally, nor any more deserving of freedom and autonomy, than are barbarians. The relationship between their value commitments and the cultural content of their psyches are, in Mill and Ms. Taylor, structurally similar Both are racists—each is equally subject to a primal bigotry; each knows racism is not "politically correct," but each nonetheless labors under the psychic weight of a cultural blindness. Their values do not cohere with the content of their own psyches.

This tension between one's avowed values and the constitution of one's historical psyche is a problem that requires more than a strong commitment to widely accepted values. That tension impedes the work of those values.

Any value commitments are filtered through historically and culturally conditioned psyches. When Ms. Taylor posts her comment about Ms. Obama, she does not see her own racism. When the Ferguson Police Department marshals military equipment against peaceful protesters, they do not see their racism; it hides behind their "law-and-order" rhetoric. When John Stuart Mill thinks of Indian natives as not civilized peoples, he does not see his own racism. Values do not implement themselves. Only individuals can implement values.

Achieving justice is not straightforward—not between or among individuals and not between or among communities. The cultural and historical limits of our moral vision are greater obstacles than we acknowledge. Frequently those limits are invisible to us.

Is Progress Possible?

Begin by recalling from the previous chapter the parts of our psyches that derive principally from Plato. Respect for authority and certainty about our value perspectives are the two most prominent Platonist results that persist in our contemporary value world. Add to these results those originating in Mill's commitment to freedom and individual autonomy. The American world is a combination of these value perspectives.

We think we *know* what is right and what justice requires. Our confidence about our own values, about rightness and justice when we judge of them, is high. Furthermore, following Mill, we believe strongly in individual freedom and autonomy. (Plato would have found this belief very strange; most individuals in his view lack the intellectual prowess that deserves autonomy.) Combining these two strands of our Western intellectual tradition yields the moral, social and political conundrums of our American world.

Our respect for others comes from our commitment to respecting their equality with ourselves; their individual autonomy is as important as our own. And we hold this commitment with powerful conviction. However, like Mill, we fail to see the limitation to these commitments posed by our own psyches.

We are historical, cultural humans who fail to see our own limitations. Like Mill, we are blind to the ways we fail to see how *certain* others deserve the same equality we naturally confer on most of our peers. We are racists in our hearts, even when we believe so strongly in our values we cannot believe otherwise.

So it was with Mill. So it was with Paula Ramsey Taylor. So it was with the Ferguson police department. And so on.

Our hope for progress, for justice in the American world, depends on our finding a way of conceiving justice differently. Justice itself needs the cooperation of our historically and culturally limited psyches. Finding a way to aim at such cooperation is the point of this book.

Consider next the thought of an American economist who elaborates Mill's liberalism specifically for the American context, Milton Friedman.

CHAPTER 5

Milton Friedman, American Economist and Liberal (1912–2006)

Abstract Milton Friedman is the twentieth-century incarnation of John Stuart Mill. Friedman was a Nobel Prize-winning University of Chicago economist who argued all of his professional life that Mill's liberalism should pervade the American moral, social and political worlds. Friedman's laissez-faire views about the economy lead him to object to the "war on drugs," one contemporary symptom of the racism pervasive in the American world. But Friedman's commitment to pure capitalism as the only legitimate way to address the racism pervasive in American culture is so naïve as itself to be racist. I argue that Friedman is as racist as Mill—and precisely because of his intellectual commitment to the liberal tradition rooted in Mill. In this chapter, as in the others, I recur frequently to controversy in the contemporary American social and political world.

Keywords Liberalism · Laissez-faire · Racism · Economics

Milton Friedman was one of the twentieth century's most prominent American economists. Friedman's commitment to classical liberalism brought him to distinctive positions on a variety of controversial social issues. The liberal tradition, best exemplified by Mill's 1859 *On Liberty*, Friedman held to be key to successful democratic institutions. In particular, government interference in individual lives and decisions must, as in Mill's thought, be minimal. Supporting and enabling individual

© The Author(s) 2018   41
S. Rosenbaum, *Race, Justice and American Intellectual Traditions*,
https://doi.org/10.1007/978-3-319-76198-5_5

freedom and autonomy must, in Friedman's view, be the primary goal of democratic government.

Friedman's 1962 *Capitalism and Freedom* is a classic twentieth-century follow-on to Mill's nineteenth-century *On Liberty*. Friedman, unlike Mill, gives specific attention to a number of current social issues and makes liberal—perhaps "libertarian" in more contemporary rhetorical garb—recommendations about them. The principle guiding Friedman's economic thought is the principle from Mill's *On Liberty* quoted in the previous chapter. Again,

> That principle is, that the sole end for which mankind are warranted, individually or collectively, in interfering with the liberty of action of any of their number, is self-protection. (Mill, John Stuart, *On Liberty*, 2003)

Where any individual's behavior does not produce harm to others, that behavior must be tolerated; such is the entire point of the individualism bequeathed to us by the Enlightenment. Both the American Revolution against the British monarchy and the French revolution against the French monarchy enabled that freedom and autonomy. Encroachments on individual freedom and autonomy by any governing authority ought not to be tolerated. Some current practices of democratic governments, however, are clear violations of that principle of classical liberalism.

Friedman enumerates a number of "socialist" style policies that have been accepted in the American world and to which he objects; those policies are clear violations of the individual freedom that should characterize democracy. The military draft is one example; the draft deprives young men of the freedom to choose their own course of life. Another example is Social Security, grounded in a payroll tax Americans must pay throughout their working lives to support a monthly annuity payment when they reach retirement age. Social Security deprives people of the freedom to make their own choices about how to spend their hard-earned money.

These examples are only two of the many Friedman mentions as violations of the individual freedom that should be an inviolable inheritance from our Enlightenment roots. Here is a lengthy quotation from *Capitalism and Freedom* that captures Friedman's commitment:

> The heart of the liberal philosophy is a belief in the dignity of the individual, in his freedom to make the most of his capacities and opportunities

according to his own lights, subject only to the proviso that he not interfere with the freedom of other individuals to do the same... .. This is an important and fundamental right precisely because men are different, because one man will want to do different things with his freedom than another, and in the process can contribute more than another to the general culture of the society in which many men live.

The liberal will therefore distinguish sharply between the equality of rights and equality of opportunity, on the one hand and material equality or equality of outcome on the other... .. He will welcome measures that promote both freedom and equality—such as measures to eliminate monopoly power and to improve the operation of the market. He will regard private charity directed at helping the less fortunate as an example of the proper use of freedom... ..

The egalitarian will go this far, too. But he will want to go further. He will defend taking from some to give to others, not as a more effective means whereby the "some" can achieve an objective they want to achieve, but on grounds of "justice." At this point, equality comes sharply into conflict with freedom; one must choose. One cannot be both an egalitarian, in this sense, and a liberal. (Friedman, Milton, 2002, 195)

Friedman is a strong advocate of Mill's liberalism in almost unadulterated form. Interference by government authorities in individual lives is *verboten*. The military draft and Social Security are only two of the common practices in recent American history that violate this fundamental principle of liberalism. Friedman is a controversial figure, even outside of economics, because of his principled adherence to Mill's principle. Laws against drug use are equal violations of that principle. Here are excerpts from a 1991 interview Friedman did with award-winning drug reporter Randy Paige:

The Proper role of government is exactly what John Stuart Mill said in the middle of the 19th century in "On Liberty." The proper role of government is to prevent other people from harming an individual. Government, he said, never has any right to interfere with an individual for that individual's own good... ..

The case for prohibiting drugs is exactly as strong and as weak as the case for prohibiting people from overeating... ..

[The drug problem is] not an economic problem at all, it's a moral problem... ... It's a problem of the harm which the government is doing. I have estimated statistically that the prohibition of drugs produces, on the average, ten thousand homicides a year. It's a moral problem that the government is going around killing ten thousand people. It's a moral problem that the government is making into criminals people, who may be doing something you and I don't approve of, but who are doing something that hurts nobody else. (Online at the American Enterprise Institute site)

Friedman's application of Mill's liberty principle is systematic. Good government respects Mill's principle, and bad government violates it. And "justice," as Friedman observes, that seeks more "equality" for the human world is a "will-o'-the-wisp"; one must choose between freedom and "justice." Justice requires controlling individuals and curtailing their freedom.

Friedman and Race

Also distinctive of Friedman's defense of the liberal principle is his application of it to issues of race. When it comes to "discrimination," Friedman believes that the only morally acceptable solution is unfettered capitalism. Forcing individuals to treat different others in some way to which they are not disposed undermines their freedom and autonomy. One should let individuals behave as they choose and let the free market change their behavior. Here are Friedman's own words:

The man who objects to buying from or working alongside a Negro, for example, thereby limits his range of choice. He will generally have to pay a higher price for what he buys or receive a lower return for his work. Or, put the other way, those of us who regard color of skin or religion as irrelevant can buy some things more cheaply as a result... ... I believe strongly that the color of a man's skin or the religion of his parents is, by itself, no reason to treat him differently; that a man should be judged by what he is and what he does and not by these external characteristics. I deplore what seem to me the prejudice and narrowness of outlook of those whose tastes differ from mine in this respect and I think the less of them for it. But in a society based on free discussion, the appropriate recourse is for me to seek to persuade them that their tastes are bad and that they should change their views and their behavior, not to use coercive power to enforce my tastes and my attitudes on others. (Friedman, Milton, *Capitalism and Freedom*, 2002, 111)

The only morally acceptable tools Friedman believes are consistent with fighting racism in a democracy are those that fully respect individual freedom. Racism, in his view, must decay and eventually die in a free capitalist economy.

Friedman does, as Mill does not, explicitly address the issue of racism. Friedman fails, however, as does Mill to appreciate the deep pathology that is racism even in capitalist democracies.

Individuals may have deep convictions—frequently religious convictions—that undermine the ideal egalitarian goal of capitalism. (Frederick Douglass, in *Narrative of the Life of an American Slave*, speaks eloquently about the support their Christian religion gave southerners for their practice of slavery.) Their religious beliefs may enable some individuals to incur with impunity even significant economic disadvantage. Racism lies "deeper" in individual psyches than is accessible by commercial transactions and their consequences. In this respect, Friedman like Mill is naive about the moral content of capitalism and liberalism. A brief and focused history of the American cultural world focused on race reveals Friedman's naivety.

Merely mention of names rooted in the history of black Americans' struggles for equality and freedom reveals the depth of racism's hold on American psyches. Frederick Douglass, Harriet Beecher Stowe, Phyllis Wheatley, W.E.B. DuBois, Martin Luther King, Jr., Emmett Till and Willie Horton evince struggles and events that continue into the contemporary world. And more recently in the twenty-first century, the names of Michael Brown, Laquan McDonald, Freddie Gray and Tamir Rice bring urgent focus to the issue of racism in America. The cumulative effect of these and the large number of additional names that come and go in our racist social world shows that racism is a deeper problem than can be addressed adequately by Enlightenment liberalism. Economic policies, even in the hands of gifted intellectuals like Friedman and Mill, do not address the deep pathologies of our racist psyches. And the inadequacies of those policies is increasingly evident in an American world in which the naivety and racism of Friedman and Mill persists. And because of more complex social and political conditions, that naivety and racism are yielding more aggressive behavior and becoming more resistant to change. But why should we take Friedman's—and Mill's—liberalism seriously as a way to address issues of racism?

What justifies Mill's liberty principle? Why should Americans accept the principle? Why should American's live by it or vote in accord with it?

These questions become especially pressing in the cultural context of American society where the liberty principle is violated by many policies and laws. Offenses against individual freedom are commonplace in American democracy, and they are accepted simply as a natural part of the American political world. Drug laws are only some of many such violations. The questions become even more pressing when one recalls Friedman's earlier-noted scoffing at the idea that "justice" might legitimate interference with individuals' freedom and autonomy.

The justification question is acute precisely because American government regularly violates, and with presumed justification and public approval, the liberty principle. Twenty-first-century Republican Party politics especially is ambivalent about Friedman's systematic commitment to Mill's principle.

"CONSERVATIVE" LIBERALISM

Liberalism is not an acceptable label in American politics. To be a "liberal" in the American political world is political suicide. At the time he published *Capitalism and Freedom* in 1962, Friedman was aware of this decline of "liberal" as a politically acceptable label; he nonetheless embraced the label because of its distinguished history and because of his own commitment to Mill's principle. The unavoidable fact of the contemporary American political world, however, is that Mill and Friedman's liberalism is no longer politically viable. "Conservatives" have appropriated Friedman's liberalism for their *economic* views and have rejected it for their social and moral views. Conservatives fight drug use, for example, as destructive of traditional values and lives, whereas Friedman finds drug use a morally acceptable, if undesirable, consequence of the liberty principle.

Following Mill and Friedman, conservatives in the contemporary American world want to make that world liberal *economically,* but conservative socially and culturally. "Liberal" has become a vague and pejorative label for those Americans who want to "tax and spend" and let the social world "go to hell in a hand-basket." "Conservative" has become an honorific label for those Americans who want to "get government off our backs" economically, but also to preserve the social and cultural values of an earlier American world.

Conservatism has become an awkward combination of Friedman's economic liberalism and the Christian social values of an earlier American world. In that earlier American world, "marriage equality" was not a possible idea; marriage just was "between one man and one woman." Men did not marry men; women did not marry women. Transgender ambitions—men wanting to become women or women wanting to become men—did not exist. And drugs and drug use were not a commonplace as they are currently (and illegally).

Conservatives these days seek to write their disgust with social developments like marriage equality and transgender mobility into laws that frustrate those developments. Which bathrooms may somebody use? Those specified for the gender written on their birth certificates is the Texas's legislature's reply. No matter how feminine a woman may appear, if her birth certificate says "male" she must use the men's bathroom. And so on for many varieties of conservative reaction to contemporary social developments.

The intellectual ambivalence of contemporary American conservatives needs explanation. What rationale or justification might yield the combination of positions that make up American conservatives' world? Mill or Friedman's liberalism will not work. Recall Friedman's principled—and liberal—defense of individual freedom of choice about the use of drugs. Marijuana or cocaine or any drug they might wish Americans should be free in Friedman's view to use. What explains this awkward inconsistency among American conservatives?

History and Values

The only possible explanation for this awkward ambivalence is historical and cultural. No clean and unambiguous principle yields the awkward combination of views that makes up "conservative" Republican Party politics. History is cultural change as much as it is political change. And value change is part of cultural change.

In the eighteenth century, for example, colonists were British and European, and brought with them their Enlightenment values, their religious values and their expectations of what might be possible in this "primitive" land. Like John Stuart Mill, the colonists divided the world into themselves as civilized and deserving, and barbarians as needing conquest and control. Native Americans were one class of such barbarians. Slaves brought from Africa to work colonists' properties were another class of barbarians. The colonists' ways of seeing the world were not as sophisticated as Mill's, but their sorting of the world's people into civilized and barbarian was just like Mill's.

Friedman follows Mill more closely than any other thinker in the twentieth century. Friedman follows Mill also in his racism. Perhaps thinking of Friedman as racist seems too aggressive, but the idea that respecting economic freedom is an adequate way to undermine the racism deeply rooted in human psyches is so naïve as to be irresponsible. That idea *is* racist. Friedman admittedly is clear about his *conscious preferences* against discrimination. *But the naivety that motivates his preferred social policy is blind to the discriminatory inertia of American culture, an inertia deeply rooted in individual psyches.*

The calls for justice that come early and repeatedly in the early twenty-first century are plaintive cries for racial equality. The brute fact that racism pervades American culture becomes evident in the multiple "incidents" of police brutality displayed on social media: the killing of Laquan McDonald in Chicago; the killing of Philando Castille in Falcon Heights, Minnesota; the killing of Walter Scott in North Charleston, South Carolina, Tamir Rice in Cleveland, Ohio and Jordan Edwards in Mesquite, Texas. And these are only a few of the more notable killings of black men by police officers in the United States. (For a more extensive listing and detailed accounts, search online for "police killings of black men.") Also contributing to the inertia of racism in American culture are the "war on drugs," segregation of communities by race, segregation of schools by race, and laws designed explicitly to make voting difficult for poor minorities, especially poor black people, and self-interested politicians eager to exploit for their own political advantage the benefits of these injustices. (In April 2017, Judge Nelva Ramos of the United States District Court for the Southern District of Texas ruled that the voter identification law the Texas legislature passed in 2011 *intended* to discriminate against black and Hispanic voters. See Manny Fernandez, *New York Times*, April 10, 2017.)

For an extensive and detailed account of these and other injustices, see Michelle Alexander, *The New Jim Crow* (New York, The New Press, 2010). Alexander gives both a coherent, large-scale picture of American racism in the early twenty-first century, as well as much detail about how that racism affects individuals. One cannot read her book without *feeling* the injustice and inequality that pervade the American world. In Alexander's view, the war on drugs is the contemporary version of the Jim Crow laws that legally enforced racial inequality during most of the twentieth century. Here are Alexander's words:

Arguably the most important parallel between mass incarceration and Jim Crow is that both have served to define the meaning and significance of race in America. Indeed, a primary function of any racial caste system is to define the meaning of race in its time. Slavery defined what it meant to be black (a slave), and Jim Crow defined what it meant to be black (a second-class citizen). Today mass incarceration defines the meaning of blackness in America: black people, especially black men, are criminals. That is what it means to be black. (Alexander, Michelle, *The New Jim Crow*, 2010)

The trappings of racism in the American world have changed. The virulent oppression that is racism in the American world has not changed.

Friedman's Enlightenment liberalism perhaps enables us to see the strangeness of American drug laws, but it does not enable us to see the social, racist pathology in them. Seeing that pathology requires *seeing* the depth of racial inequality in America. Enlightenment liberalism may empower the capitalism embedded in American democracy, but it cannot empower the ideals of equality and justice that motivate many American psyches. Our shared racism is too deeply rooted in individuals and in society to respond to Friedman's too facile resort to capitalism.

But if the liberalism of Enlightenment philosophy is inadequate, might a competing, and still principled, approach more adequately address the deep racism in America? John Rawls, an American political philosopher, offers a principled alternative to Friedman's Enlightenment liberalism.

CHAPTER 6

John Rawls, American Philosopher (1921–2002)

Abstract John Rawls is the most important American philosopher who works with the idea of justice. Rawls departs definitively from the liberal tradition of Mill and Friedman and looks more like a democratic socialist in his understanding of justice. Rawls's problems with justice are twofold. (1) Rawls tries for Plato-style rational legitimation of his principles of justice. In this effort, Rawls fails. (2) Rawls, like Plato, Mill and Friedman before him, is likewise a racist. Making this case about Rawls is a bit more difficult, probably because of Rawls's intense focus on *theory*. Nevertheless, his focus on theory does not relieve Rawls of responsibility to confront real injustices of daily life. Rawls's focus on theory is no excuse and, like Mill and Friedman before him, Rawls too is a racist.

Keywords Original position · Democratic socialism · Theory Charles S. Mills

John Rawls is perhaps the best-known political philosopher of the twentieth century. Rawls saw the "Achilles Heel" of Mill and Friedman's liberalism, and he saw that justice was not an ideal that must compete with individual freedom and autonomy. In Rawls's view, justice must be integral to those values; unlike Friedman, Rawls sees no incoherence between full freedom, full autonomy and full justice. Rawls's task, as he saw it, was to formulate an alternative to the liberalism of Mill

© The Author(s) 2018   51
S. Rosenbaum, *Race, Justice and American Intellectual Traditions*,
https://doi.org/10.1007/978-3-319-76198-5_6

and Friedman that was just as plausible, rational and compelling as their liberalism had been.

Rawls's *A Theory of Justice*, 1971, may be the most important theoretical book on justice and democracy published in the latter half of the twentieth century. Rawls there formulates and defends his alternative to the liberalism of Mill and Friedman. The crux of Rawls's alternative is the two principles of justice that remain central to his thought throughout his work. Here is an early version of the two principles:

1. *The Liberty Principle*: Each person is to have an equal right to the most extensive liberty compatible with a like liberty for all.
2. *The Difference Principle*: Social and economic inequalities (as defined by the institutional structure or fostered by it) are to be arranged so that they are both to everyone's advantage and attached to positions and offices open to all.
(Rawls, John, "The Obligation to Obey the Law." 1988)

These formulations of the two principles of justice are early, appearing even before *A Theory of Justice*. The principles change in their formulations over the years of Rawls's work, but they remain in principle an alternative to the liberty principle of Mill and Friedman. (An approximation of Mill and Friedman's principle receives a contemporary philosophical defense by Rawls's colleague at Harvard, Robert Nozick in *Anarchy, State and Utopia*, 1974.)

Recall that neither Mill nor Friedman offers *argument* in favor of the liberty principle. (Mill does, as I noted, offer arguments in favor of freedom of speech and discussion, but these arguments do not cover his claim that his liberty principle should be *absolute*.) Rawls, in contrast, seeks a comprehensive philosophical defense of the two principles of justice. Justification by rational argument remains in philosophy the standard way to make plausible any principle or principles that aspire to legitimate human practice or behavior. In this respect, Rawls remains wedded to the ideal of Platonism that requires *intellectual justification* as a prerequisite for proper practice or behavior; without such justification—the sort sought in Plato's dialogues—one inevitably falls into error. (In *Political Liberalism*, 1993, Rawls modifies his early commitment to Plato-style rational justification for the two principles, though he remains committed to their substance in slightly different formulations.)

Justification of Rawls's Principles

Rawls believes the two principles are those that "free and rational men would agree to in an original position of equal liberty"; they are "the outcome of a hypothetical agreement." The agreement in question must occur in an "original position" of relative innocence in which individuals do not know their own particular interests. Individuals in the original position do not know their gender, their race, their talents or lack thereof, their intelligence or lack thereof, their social position, their most fundamental values or the circumstances in which they will live. Individuals know only that they are choosing principles under which they agree to live. Rawls's instinct is that in this original position of innocence, all would choose to live according to the two principles of justice. The hypothetical character of the original position—nobody having the ability to choose is ever in such circumstances of innocence—yields intellectual difficulties for it.

What principles *would you* choose to live by in Rawls's original position of innocence? Is a choice of those two principles of justice the only *proper* or *rational* choice for you? Or is that choice perhaps a function of how adventuresome or risk-averse you might be? The results of Rawls's hypothetical original position fall prey to diversities inherent in personality and character; some of us humans—even when we are rational and behind the "veil of ignorance" implicit in Rawls's original position—are more adventurous or more risk-averse than others. Might you not prefer to live according to the liberty principle defended so ably by Mill and Friedman? If you lived in a society where that liberty principle controlled human relationships, you would have a chance of coming out "on top," being among the "one percent" perhaps, or at least among the top ten percent. No agreement on the best answer to the question posed in the original position is forthcoming. Does this result mean Rawls's principles of justice are simply his own preference? Does it mean those principles are entirely optional and lack proper justification?

Of course not. Rawls's principles capture fundamentally important values of our democratic world. Those principles are expressions of vital aspiration for a democratic world that remains elusive, even in the most vigorously democratic of Western societies. Those principles are an expression of the unity of the values of freedom, equality, autonomy and justice, the fundamental values of the contemporary Western world. How to realize the harmony of those values is *the* problem of Western democracies. Rawls's near obsession with the project of *justifying* those values expresses his realization that such harmony is a basic condition of successful democracy. Some individuals will be more successful in an autocracy or an oligarchy, but democracy, as Rawls sees, requires greater equality and justice of economic relationships than can be realized under those other institutional arrangements. And Rawls does back away from his efforts at *philosophical justification* of those principles of justice and in later work, like *Political Liberalism*, begins seeing them more like the principles we *should* choose if we are serious about our democratic aspirations.

The justification issue never disappears in Rawls's work, but it takes a different form, even a "back seat," as he struggles with the realization that there may be no epistemically secure foundation for our most vital Western values. Still, Rawls sees the basic significance of those values for our democratic world; he sees that justice must be integral to our commitments to liberty and autonomy, and he urges that justice be integrated into our thought about democracy. Rawls sees the inevitable fault in a democracy narrowly focused on the freedom and autonomy prominent in Mill, Friedman and in much of the contemporary political world.

Perhaps one should notice also that the coherence Rawls sees among freedom, autonomy and justice is not prominent in the American Revolution or in its founding documents, the Declaration of Independence of 1776 and the Constitution of 1787. Those founding documents emphasize freedom and autonomy, as do Mill and Friedman, but they are blind to the justice that Rawls sees must be integral to successful democracy; in this respect, those documents are Enlightenment documents in their emphasis on individual freedom and autonomy. Those founding documents, however, share the same racial blindness that infects the work of Mill and Friedman, and they make difficult (especially for "strict constitutionalists") integrating the idea of justice into the institutional structures of American democracy. Other Western democracies do not have the same difficulty.

The French revolution of 1789, for example, embodies not just the American commitment to freedom and equality, but also to *fraternity*. Adding fraternity as an equal partner for the values of freedom and equality enables significant institutional possibility in France that is not available in the American (strictly) constitutional world. Notice, for example, that some historical decisions of the American Supreme Court rigidly adhere to the explicit American constitutional values of freedom and equality, and some "err" in the direction of fraternity or justice, conceived approximately as Rawls does.

The Affordable Care Act, signed by President Obama in 2010, embodies implicitly the values of fraternity and justice. At his signing of the bill, President Obama said that it affirms "the core principle that everybody should have some basic security when it comes to... health care." One question that exposes the conflict of values over the ACA is, why should anybody be legally required to purchase health insurance or pay a fine for their refusal to do so? Perhaps, as President Obama said, everybody should have basic health care, but perhaps only if they choose to purchase it? Federally mandating a purchase of health insurance is an obvious violation of individual autonomy, and on that score such a mandate is objectionable. When, however, the mandate is part of an arrangement whereby more health-care needy individuals, perhaps having preexisting conditions, are able to purchase health care, then the mandate becomes more reasonable from a standpoint that emphasizes justice and fraternity. The mandate that healthier, younger individuals purchase health insurance spreads the costs over a larger group and makes insurance more affordable for those who are more needy. Thus considered, the mandate is an expression of the values of fraternity or justice, even though it is an evident violation of the freedom and autonomy that are central to Mill, Friedman and our founding fathers.

(As I review this manuscript before sending the final version to the publisher I note that President Trump has signed a tax reform bill that eliminates the individual mandate to purchase health insurance prescribed by the Affordable Care Act, by "Obamacare." The Republican House and Senate removed that mandate as part of their tax reform legislation, thereby providing confirmation of my thesis about contemporary Republican politics. For more relevant material about this issue, see Part II below, especially Chapter 9.)

The controversy surrounding the Affordable Care Act makes evident the conflict of basic values always inherent in the world of politics. Those basic values usually are covered over with distorting rhetoric—as, for example, the common accusation against "Obamacare" that it is "a job-killer"—even though the most fundamental, and frequently unvoiced, objection to it is that it too strongly emphasizes the values of justice and fraternity over those of freedom and autonomy. These tensions are a part of American political reality. Constitutional challenges to the Affordable Care Act make perfect sense when seen through the lens of these conflicts of value.

The liberty principle of Mill and Friedman conflicts historically with Rawls's two principles of justice and with the value of fraternity embodied in the French revolution. Rawls's conviction is that the historical conflict of those principles and values is not inherent or inevitable; those principles and values may cooperate harmoniously in a future, democratic world.

Freedom and autonomy, combined with justice and fraternity, are values for a fuller democratic future. The Enlightenment values embodied in the American constitution must find a way to live comfortably with the European democratic ideals that more fully embody fraternity and justice. Rawls is an American beacon shining toward that possibility.

RAWLS AND RACE

Rawls's effort to bring the values of justice and fraternity more fully into the American democratic world is laudable, though it remains controversial in American politics largely because of America's founding, *Enlightenment* documents. From the standpoint of ordinary social concerns about justice, however, Rawls's lifelong commitment to just democratic institutions is little helpful.

When black citizens of Ferguson, Missouri plea for justice for Michael Brown, little of Rawls's intense concern about justice touches the realities of their situation. Those citizens of American democracy see themselves as second-class citizens whom the police do not respect or treat equally; they feel themselves targeted, singled out, for discriminatory treatment as less than full American citizens. And they believe too that Michael Brown suffered injustice and unequal treatment. Police officers they believe discriminate unjustly against them by treating them as less than fully equal American citizens. Had Michael Brown been a white American, they believe, Darren Wilson would not have shot and killed him. They see racism in Wilson's action.

Rawls's concern to make justice and fairness central to American democracy misses what the black citizens of Ferguson feel about their unjust mistreatment by the white police officers of their community. The moral and social concerns of those black citizens most of their racial peers in the American world also share. (Recall the small sample mentioned in chapter one of other cases of white police abuse and killing of black men and boys.)

Perhaps Rawls, like Mill and Friedman, has a cultural "blind spot?" Perhaps Rawls, again like Mill and Friedman, is racist? How does one *see*, or *fail to see*, failures of equality and justice when these are commonplace in daily media outlets and on social media? Rawls's philosophical concerns are, like those of Plato, Mill and Friedman with institutional structures; those structures can function well or badly, can be fair or unfair, just or unjust in their workings. Perhaps all these thinkers are innocent of racism? Perhaps their intellectual concerns about justice are "structural" and thus different from and independent of the concerns of the citizens of Ferguson? Perhaps Rawls does *see* the unjust and unequal treatment of black American citizens and, like Friedman, regrets that injustice and inequality?

Judgments that any given individual is racist admittedly are difficult. Such judgments are difficult not least because judging somebody racist is charging them with moral defect. (All Americans acknowledge at this point in history the immorality of slavery, and almost all Americans acknowledge the immorality of racism. Recall Paula Ramsey Taylor's impassioned defense of herself after her "tweet" about Michelle Obama occasioned accusations of racism against her.)

Does Rawls's intellectual concern with justice relieve him of the intellectual responsibility to address concerns like those of the citizens of Ferguson? And can Rawls thereby be spared the embarrassment of being charged with racism at the heart of his intellectual work? These questions are difficult, and they are difficult for the same reason asking such questions about anybody are difficult: almost all of us acknowledge the immorality of racism. But we can *see* the racism in Paula Ramsey Taylor's tweet about Michelle Obama, and why should we not see a similar defect in the intellectual concerns of John Rawls?

Perhaps like Ms. Taylor, Rawls is unaware of relevant contents of his own psyche? We can see the racism in Mill's attitude toward natives of the Indian subcontinent. We can see the racism in Friedman's naïve claim that capitalism will suffice to orient our moral world properly as regards our "discriminative" tendencies. Why should we not make that same judgment about John Rawls?

At this point, the only obstacle to our thinking of Rawls as, like Mill and Friedman, racist is Rawls's insistence that his concerns are with social and moral theory, with the social structure of an ideal democracy. Rawls does not see himself as racist. But neither did Paula Ramsey Taylor. In our understandings of our own psyches, we are all innocent of moral offense. And especially are we innocent of such egregious moral offense as racism!

We must, in honesty and fairness, acknowledge that subterranean dimensions of our own psyches are opaque to ourselves. We must depend on others who know us and understand us to let us know when we stray from the values we avow. About this fundamental fact of our conscious lives psychologists have long known; each of us is naturally, and likely in fundamental ways, "hypocritical." (For accessible accounts of this fundamental fact, see Malcolm Gladwell *Blink*, 2005, and Daniel Kahneman, *Thinking Fast and Slow*, 2011.)

If the judgment of racism against Paula Ramsey Taylor makes sense; and if the judgments of racism against Mill and Friedman make sense; then that same judgment likely makes sense against Rawls as well. In proposing the charge of racism against Rawls, I have been circumspect to a fault; I have refrained from claims that might be offensive to Rawls or to fellow moral philosophers engaged in specifying the social/political structure of an ideal democratic world. Consider now the explicit charges of one who is not so circumspect. Charles W. Mills explicitly argues that Rawls is a racist in "Rawls on Race/Race in Rawls," a lively and disconcerting essay from 2009.

Mills on Rawls

Mills pulls no punches when discussing Rawls's account of justice. Rawls is straightforwardly racist, according to Mills, and is so because of his willingness to locate his concern with justice fully within the classical Western intellectual tradition. That Western intellectual tradition is, in Mills's and in my own view, thoroughly racist. John Stuart Mill and Milton Friedman are only two of the thinkers who supply roots for Rawls's racism. Mills becomes in this essay one of those others I earlier mentioned on whom we depend to reveal contents of our psyches that may otherwise remain hidden to ourselves. We depend on each other not only for many social and personal needs, but also for insights into the contents of our own psyches.

Western political—and social, moral, epistemological and metaphysical—theory assumes European, white supremacy. Western political theory, whether in Hobbes, Locke, Mill or Rawls is deeply—and imperceptibly to Western psyches—racist.

For five centuries and more, European colonialism subjected the native peoples of the entire globe to conquest and domination. That domination rested on a presumption of European—and "white"—cultural, moral and metaphysical superiority. This presumption was for centuries, and remains largely unquestioned; it was a given for all European psyches, and was embedded in all European cultures as much as was the idea that monarchs were God's representatives on earth or as was later the Enlightenment idea that reason was an authoritative source for knowledge about morality and society.

This cultural situation did not acknowledge—did not even recognize—in its colonialist appropriations of native lands and peoples any racist intent. The racism of those European cultures Europeans themselves simply could not conceive, since the "inferiority" of conquered and dominated native peoples was undisputed even in their imaginations. Political and moral theory—as well as other modes of theory—were rooted in assumptions of European, and white, superiority. And those assumptions were hidden from their/our own psyches.

(An interesting analogue of the racism hidden in European psyches is the anthropocentricism hidden in all modes of explanation prior to the scientific revolution of the seventeenth century. During prior centuries Aristotelian-style teleological explanation *just was* explanation, and it modeled goal-directed explanations of human behavior. Thus, each basic element in Aristotle's "table of elements" had a "natural place" in the universe where it belonged and a simple, single desire to get there in the most direct way possible. This Aristotelian anthropocentricism changed definitively during the seventeenth century, culminating in the Newtonian physics that made Aristotelian teleology no longer scientifically reputable. After Newton, scientific explanation became utterly detached, impersonal and "objective," involving only matter in motion and the mechanical laws that govern that motion.)

John Stuart Mill, along with his European intellectual fellows, could not *see* their racism. Racism did not exist for them. Mill and his fellows did see social scaffolding, but they did not see native peoples as falling anywhere on the scaffold they and their European colleagues sought to rationalize. Native peoples were "other," uncivilized, barbarians, and these native peoples included Africans, Indians, Native Americans and others. Here is one way Mills puts this disturbing fact:

> The fact is—unthinkable as it may be within Rawls's framework of assumptions—that in a sense all the Western European nations (and their offshoots, such as the United States) were "outlaw states" jointly involved in a criminal enterprise on a planetary scale. (Mills, Charles W., "Rawls on Race/Race in Rawls," 2009, 171)

The colonialism of Western Europeans rested on a racism the Europeans themselves simply *could not see*. And no more could their European descendants—The United States, Australia and others—see their racism. The intellectual elite within these European states, along with their progeny, likewise were/are unable to see their own racism.

John Rawls, despite his otherwise noble intentions, shares the racism of his cultural and intellectual ancestors. "Ideal theory," that noble moral, social and epistemologically respectable goal, falls under the weight of its own racism. Not to see, not to notice, not to mind the racist albatross hanging from the neck of ideal theory is implicitly to confess one's own racism. Like Mill and Friedman before him—and like Paula Ramsey Taylor—Rawls is a racist.

Rawls's work on justice and democracy is surely among the more creative and compelling intellectual achievements of the Western world of the twentieth century. Our conclusion here, nonetheless, must be that like Mill and Friedman before him, Rawls too has a significant cultural limitation, a "blindness" to palpable injustices that his monumental work on justice does not address. How may we think about justice in yet more comprehensive a way that overcomes limitations in the thought of these giants of Western intellectual culture? How may we escape, or address constructively, the cultural blindness embedded in their thought?

CHAPTER 7

Retrospect and More

Abstract This chapter is a summary account of the content of previous chapters and reinforces the point that Western intellectual culture, especially in its American incarnation, is thoroughly racist. I augment the summary dimension of this chapter with brief historical comments on ideology, race and genocide. The genocide carried out against Natives of "the New World" was founded on the intellectual, religious and moral traditions of the Western world discussed in preceding chapters.

Keywords Genocide · Racism · Ideology · Indigenous

Chapter 2 showed us that justice, at least in the Western tradition, lives in individuals as a universal and absolute idea. We *see* the basic moral truths that impregnate our lives and circumstances, and we make moral judgments about others and about our circumstances in light of those truths. Our confidence in our moral vision is undaunted by disagreements with others.

When others disagree about our moral judgments, we explain their disagreement by their "clouded vision," by their defect of moral character. Some people, we reason, may be good people who are simply deprived in some way of the clarity of vision with which we are blessed. Likely those good people are bigots of some sort, frequently racists, who are deprived by their defective moral character of their ability to see what we see so clearly.

© The Author(s) 2018 61
S. Rosenbaum, *Race, Justice and American Intellectual Traditions*,
https://doi.org/10.1007/978-3-319-76198-5_7

The circumstances of the killing of Michael Brown by Darren Wilson suggest murder to some of us. To others, Darren Wilson was properly defending himself in shooting Brown. Such disagreements—remember the introductory philosophy class—are common in the American social world.

Not only our idea of justice but also our belief that many others are deprived of clarity of moral vision by their defective characters are embedded in our standard ways of thinking about justice—and about morality in general.

PLATO

Chapter 3 showed us the origin of some of our most basic ideas about value and justice. We share with Plato the idea that those we trust for our value opinions are genuinely authoritative, that they are proper stewards of our opinions and behavior. Accordingly, we hold those opinions with conviction. As did Plato, we repose almost perfect confidence in our value opinions. And like Plato, we repose confidence in those external authorities we trust—though unlike Plato, our authorities do not include reason itself. Our authorities are a bit closer to our human worlds and include religious authorities and religious texts.

Where justice is concerned, however, we share Plato's conviction that it is *one*, that it is knowable and absolute and *the same* for anybody anywhere. Our individualism, however, leads us to different authoritative sources for our value opinions and behaviors.

Some of us believe abortion is murder and is thus obviously morally wrong; others of us believe abortion is morally acceptable in some circumstances. And so on with any controversial issue. We acknowledge this variation of moral opinion, though we nevertheless continue to believe, as Plato would have us do, that only one opinion—always ours—is correct. The absolutism of Plato remains firmly embedded in our Western moral world.

Frequently, however, we must act in the absence of authoritative external guidance, as in the confrontation between Michael Brown and Darren Wilson. Even though no external authority is available in such situations, we do rely on "internal resources" rooted in our characters. These resources do not come to us with the same clarity as do our external authorities, but they usually do come to us with the same measure of confidence as do our opinions and behaviors derived from Pope, Bible or Koran. We trust ourselves. Our trust in ourselves in such situations coheres with our democratic individualism.

Platonism finds its way only partially into our individualistic post-Enlightenment world. But the parts of Platonism that do remain are strong.

MILL

The liberal traditions of the American world find their most vigorous statement in the work of John Stuart Mill, and especially in *On Liberty*. The principle defended in Mill finds political realization in the American Constitution of 1787. That principle's basic value commitment is to individual freedom and individual autonomy. Mill's commitment to those values, however, is qualified by his reserving of them for "civilized peoples."

Mill's work for the East India Company may have affected his approach to his intellectual commitments, for he found no conflict between his value commitments to individual freedom and autonomy along with his official denial of them to natives of the Indian subcontinent.

Mill's view that non-civilized people do not have the same rights as civilized people is evidence of a racism—or some primal bigotry or xenophobia perhaps more subtle than the label "racism" suggests—that escaped his own awareness. Those primal, discriminatory attitudes find their way into every culture, and even the brightest and best of any culture do not escape them. Mill's earnest work is perhaps the best evidence one might have for this claim.

FRIEDMAN

The continuity between serious intellectual value commitments and implicit racist attitudes appears also in the work of this Nobel Prize-winning American economist. Friedman is one of the more idealistic of theorists, in the sense that he sincerely believes that individual freedom and autonomy are *the* values that should be realized in American democracy. When, however, he turns to an explicit discussion of racism in the American world, he does not see his own failure.

Racist attitudes are much more deeply embedded in individuals' character than might be addressed by the simple nostrum, "let the free market work its miracle in racist psyches." Individuals have convictions.

Individuals feel duty-bound to uphold their convictions. Paying more for a product, out of the conviction that one should *not* treat sellers of goods equally when those sellers are of different races, is an acceptable sacrifice. Capitalism and freedom and autonomy are not solutions to the racism deeply embedded in American psyches. More is required.

Although Friedman scorns "justice" as a proper value alongside freedom and autonomy, those values are not sufficient to realize the potential of a genuinely democratic world in which justice and fraternity are equals of freedom and autonomy.

RAWLS

Rawls realizes the limitations of the principled commitments of Mill and Friedman, and seeks to bring justice into the center of democracy. Even though the American Constitution, an Enlightenment document, does not recognize the need for justice and fraternity among all citizens, Rawls understands that they are indispensible to successful democracy. Rawls too, however, has limitations when it comes to the issue of racism, and he fails to see the difficulties involved in getting the unity of those democratic values *into* citizens. Rawls does not see the intellectual content of the idea of justice as intimately involved in the *practices* of communities that use that idea in their own value worlds.

Rawls mentions race only rarely, and then only as giving rise to immoral institutions like slavery. A theory of justice, in Rawls's view, need not dwell on immoral historical aberrations but rather on ideal institutional arrangements that might in principle be realized in contemporary democracies. Although Rawls acknowledges immoralities like slavery, racism and imperialism, he does not believe that his theory of justice need be especially concerned with those issues. Rawls is giving account of principles and institutions that would enable realization of ideal democracies. As do the other thinkers mentioned in previous chapters, Rawls is giving account of an *ideal*.

AGAIN

Plato's ideal is a society in which those who know are completely in charge of social arrangements, and their knowledge is achieved through intellectual gifts that others lack. Mill's ideal society is one in which civilized peoples have freedom and autonomy to carry on their lives according to their own judgments about how to live; barbarians, children and incompetents are excluded. Friedman largely shares Mill's view about the ideal society, one in which individual autonomy is the highest value. And in Rawls's work, the two principles of justice show how ideal democratic institutions might function. The disagreement among these thinkers settles on the issue of what values *should* be central to ideal societies. In each of these thinkers, however, a blindness to issues of race is inseparable from their thought.

How, in any ideal society, ought one to deal with the racism persisting in citizens? How, in ideal societies, should one deal with the persistent killing of black men and boys by white policemen? The idea of just social institutions and how they might be achieved is important, but the idea of justice pertains also (and perhaps primarily) to realities of contemporary social worlds. How should one address racist realities of the contemporary world? None of these thinkers is attuned to this crucial question, and their description of ideal societies misses—is even blind to—the realities of social life in the human world.

What we must see is that concerns with justice, whether as an idea about the ideal functioning of democratic institutions or an idea about relations between and among individuals, need not and should not be divided up into "different kinds" of concern, theoretical and practical. Justice, one might say, is justice, a virtue of institutions, relationships *and* of individuals. Justice must be continuous in thought, in practice and in life; it is the same virtue both of institutions and of individuals. (In this way, Plato's claim that justice in the state and justice in the individual are mirror images of one another is on the right track.) Justice is one. But what is that one that justice is? This question is Plato's, and pursuing it in independence of the realities of society and humanity—as do Mill, Friedman and Rawls—is unproductively to segregate theory from practice. We must find a way to avoid this Platonist conundrum and its interminable elaborations.

Indeed, even in "ideal theory" one must begin with one's "intuitions" about real-world behaviors, practices and institutions. And even Plato attended to the real world of merchants, politicians, women and slaves in which he lived, and in that diverse world even Plato began theorizing with basic intuitions about justice. One selects among intuitions those one feels most accurately capture a preferred ideal, and one sees those intuitions as foundational for one's theorizing, for one's idealizing. Thus, Rawls saw that Mill and Friedman's understanding of an ideal society left out something he regarded as vitally important. That something he sought to capture in the two principles of justice. *A Theory of Justice* is an elaboration of the kind of world those two principles enable. And that world is very different from the ideal world imagined by Friedman, Mill, Ayn Rand and Paul Ryan. Both of those worlds are ideal worlds, but very different ones. And both of those ideal worlds are very different from Plato's ideal world. Who is to say, and how might one say, which of those worlds is "better" or "best?" Both are ideal worlds, different kinds of utopia imagined and argued for by different philosophers or theorists.

The different starting points of different theorists enable different ideal institutions or different ideals of human relationship. Might any starting place for ideal theory enable overcoming intractable differences among theorists? My claim here is that no starting point enables that overcoming. (I must at this point leave this claim undefended beyond simply pointing vaguely to the historical and social reality of intractable theoretical difference, along with the pervasive Platonist dispositions that pervade our Western intellectual worlds.)

How is continuity of theory and practice concerning justice possible? How may one recognize and explain that continuity apart from the trappings of Platonism that persist in the Western world? An answer to that question is the promise of Part II.

ONCE MORE: IDEOLOGY AND RACISM

Ideology and racism are twins, and the firstborn is ideology. Ideology and genocide are twins, and again the firstborn is ideology. The metaphor is unimportant, but it captures a significant relationship.

Where racism and genocide appear in our human worlds, they are functions of some motivating ideology. Without a motivating ideology, racism or other social pathologies do not manifest in our social worlds.

Stephen Ambrose, in *The Victors*, 1999, tells the story of a wounded German officer taken prisoner by American troops in their 1944 push toward Berlin and the defeat of Germany. The German officer needed a blood transfusion. When the officer asked for a guarantee that the blood he would receive was not Jewish and was denied that guarantee, he refused the transfusion and died from his wounds. To that German officer, his purity was more important than his life. The officer believed that Aryans are superior and refused to sully his own body with Jewish impurities. Ideology, for that officer, was supreme; even his life was a proper sacrifice to it.

And Frederick Douglass, in *Narrative of the Life of an American Slave*, 2001, explains how their deep religious views motivated slave-owners' views about the inferiority of their slaves. The owners' Christian, Biblical commitments gave them permission for, even mandated, their owning of slaves and their brutal treatment of those slaves. Again, their ideology triumphed over their humanity; for them, slavery and the inferiority of blacks were near the heart of their religious commitments.

Another, even more disturbing, example is the American holocaust that cleared the way for our European ancestors in the new world. After Columbus's "discovery" of America, our European ancestors wrought unprecedented brutality against Native Americans. The Spanish and the English, in particular, were guilty of crimes against humanity on such a scale as boggles the mind. Many millions of innocent Native Americans were killed and maimed beyond our ability to understand, and all for the greater glory of God. David Stannard details these egregious offenses to our contemporary sensibilities in *American Holocaust*, 1992.

The Nazi officer, the slave owners and the invading Europeans were committed intellectually to views that required their behaviors and practices; their ideology controlled their behaviors and ways of life. These earnest individuals we now see to have been seriously benighted, even morally repugnant. But their modes of arriving at their commitments and actions remain normative in our Western worlds. We embrace what we believe to be true and we apply it in our personal lives as best we can. We are, in this straightforward way, ideologues. And too, this way of arriving at our behaviors remains solidly within our Platonist tradition of thought about how to live. We diverge from Plato, of course, in our individualistic ways of appropriating our authorities—some of us are Nazis, some are slaveholders, some are white supremacists, some are antiabortion activists, some are zealous Muslims or evangelical Christians, and so on—though we remain nevertheless committed to applying our ideologies in our lives as thoroughly as we can. How else are we to live? What can we do other than know the truth and apply it in our lives?

An Italian song bears the title, "Dare to Live." A line from the song, translated into English, is "There's no one truth; there's only faces." (I assume the line in some way derives from Emmanuel Levinas's philosophical work on faces. See, e.g., Craig, Megan, *Levinas and James*, 2010.) The line suggests an alternative way to think about how to live. The alternative, roughly and vaguely put, is *live toward the faces you see about you.*

(In Stannard's account of Native Americans in *American Holocaust*, one has the impression that this vague alternative was the approximate goal of life for Native Americans before the European invasion.) The suggestion is vague at best, but it has at least the advantage of abandoning the Platonism that constrains our thought about how to live our lives. And it has also the advantage of putting our humanity before our intellect and the authorities that control it. Again, more questions: How might one do *that*?

Seeking an answer to that question, again, is the goal of Part II.

PART II

Our Problem, Our Responsibility, Our Future

CHAPTER 8

Michael Sandel's Insight

Abstract Michael Sandel sees that justice has little content of its own apart from some understanding of the good. Sandel sees that the mistake of previous thinkers—including Rawls—was thinking justice had a content all its own that could be discerned and acted upon. This insight of Sandel was already a staple of indigenous American thought and philosophy long before Sandel wrote. Sandel does see, however, the serious vulnerabilities of current American social reality and knows that conventional appeals to justice itself are useless. Sandel focuses on wealth inequality and the American need for "a politics of moral engagement." (The idea of a politics of moral engagement is too vague to be helpful, and Sandel does little to fill it out.)

Keywords Justice · The good · Moral engagement · Wealth inequality

Michael Sandel has recently given us an alternative way of thinking about issues of justice. Sandel's recent book, *Justice: What's the Right Thing to Do?* moves beyond the idea that a principle or principles about rightness or justice can yield conclusions about what a just action or democracy must look like. In Mill, in Friedman and in Rawls, justice comes from discerning intellectually—as Plato would have us do—the proper, best or correct way of thinking about justice, whether as a virtue of institutions or as a virtue of individuals. Sandel sees that this quasi-Platonist approach misses much of the heart of the matter about just institutions and just behavior.

© The Author(s) 2018   71
S. Rosenbaum, *Race, Justice and American Intellectual Traditions*,
https://doi.org/10.1007/978-3-319-76198-5_8

Sandel believes that the idea of justice has little content of its own apart from some specific understanding of what a good life is. Understandings of the good life vary from community to community and depend for their content on many variables; in addition, individuals, because of their divergent constitutions, have different understandings of *their own* good, of the kind of life *they* deem worth pursuing. To acknowledge the relevance to the idea of justice of these variations from community to community and from individual to individual is to confess that justice *itself* has little if any content of its own.

Sandel aligns himself with those in the recent philosophical world whom we think of as communitarians, and he cites Alasdair McIntyre as following suggestions in Aristotle (mentioned briefly in Chapter 3) and a prominent communitarian. (See McIntyre, Alastair, *After Virtue*, 1981.) Communitarians believe that justice itself cannot be accessed by intellect alone, for it like all other values has deep roots in the various communities that sustain us. Whether we are Catholic, Protestant, Muslim or Buddhist we have our value lives *as* members of those communities. And not just religious communities perform this essential service for us; so too do all the various communities of which we are members.

Our little league teams, our schools, our senior choirs, our fishing buddies, our gun clubs, our reading groups and other associations are constitutive of our basic values, of our understanding of the good for ourselves and others. Our responses to the various situations we encounter are in subtle ways functions of the values rooted in and shared by these and all the groups that come together in our characters. Communitarians embrace these community groups as largely constitutive of our value psyches, as enabling our various character-rooted possibilities of response in all the situations we confront.

This communitarian thought does have its roots in Aristotle rather than in Plato. However, when we think of Aristotle as a "virtue theorist," we do so not primarily because he emphasizes our community life in his thinking about morality, but rather because he believes a *certain* kind of life is primarily (or even alone) worth living, the life of intellectual activity. The intellectual life alone in Aristotle's thought is the highest goal of human life. This aiming at the single best ideal of human life—the *telos* of human life—is essential to virtue theory. Apart from that specific aim at the *telos* of human life, *nothing theoretically distinctive attends virtue theory*. Sociologists and psychologists are equally adept at pointing out the formative dimensions of community and family for our values, but they are not *virtue theorists*.

In this respect, Plato's mentoring of Aristotle has its full impact on Aristotle's thought. Aristotle's wisdom, from our perspective, extends only to his acknowledging the human roots of human values, not to his adulation of the intellect as the ultimate source of wisdom and satisfaction, and as the *telos* of human life. In this respect, Aristotle remains a footnote to Plato. (Recall that in Chapter 3, I mentioned Emerson's observation that Aristotle "Platonizes.")

Acknowledging the human roots of human values, as does McIntyre and as does Sandel, is not thereby to be a "virtue theorist"; virtue theory requires an account of *the* good of human life. Being a virtue theorist requires holding on to that continuing remnant of Platonism. Fortunately, Sandel does not—like many inclined to sympathy with communitarians because of their social realism about values—embrace the Platonism in virtue theory, its insistence that there is such a singular thing as *the* good life.

Not embracing the Platonism in virtue theory, or in most versions of communitarianism, is helpful toward the progress that enables us to make sense of *our* value world, especially our understanding of justice. Recall the story of Solomon's just adjudication of the dispute between the two women claiming the same child. And recall our American rejection of "ivory tower" intellectuals—those Americans and Westerners Plato and Aristotle would most value and appreciate—and our respect for the wisdom of Forrest Gump. Plato and Aristotle, along with their value heirs in our intellectual world, we must learn to see beyond. Sandel helps us along this constructive path in his less-than-Aristotelian communitarian perspective. Sandel's sympathy with virtue theory does not extend to Aristotle's Platonizing. Here is what Sandel says about how we must respect the contextual, community dimensions of our lives that elude the intellectualizing of our Western Platonism.

> To achieve a just society we have to reason together about the meaning of the good life, and to create a public culture hospitable to the disagreements that will inevitably arise.

It is tempting to seek a principle or procedure that could justify, once and for all, whatever distribution of income or power or opportunity resulted from it. Such a principle, if we could find it, would enable us to avoid the tumult and contention that arguments about the good life invariably arouse. (*Editorial note*: This paragraph is Sandel's rejection of Aristotle's Platonizing.)

But these arguments are impossible to avoid. <u>Justice is inescapably judgmental</u>. Whether we're arguing about financial bailouts or Purple Hearts, surrogate motherhood or same-sex marriage, affirmative action or military service, CEO pay or the right to use a golf cart, questions of justice are bound up with competing notions of honor and virtue, pride and recognition. Justice is not only about the right way to distribute things. It is also about the right way to value things. (Sandel, Michael, *Justice: What's the Right Thing to Do?* 2009, 261)

Consider, as Sandel suggests, how we might reason together in some specific cases.

In the case of marriage equality—"same-sex marriage" was the term of choice when Sandel published in 2009—feelings are and long have been intense on both sides. Clear principles fortify both sides in the intensity of their convictions.

One principle opposing marriage equality is the tradition, claimed as biblically rooted, of marriage as a sacred relationship between one man and one woman. This tradition easily transforms into the principle that marriage simply is a sacred relationship between one man and one woman commanded by God.

A principle supporting marriage equality is that individuals who love another person of the same gender have equal right to the same legal recognition as do those who love a person of the opposite sex. The 14th Amendment's guarantee of equal rights under the law applies to individuals who want to marry another person of the same sex. (This reasoning was approximately that of the majority of the Supreme Court in their 5-4 ruling in *Obergefell v Hodges*, the case guaranteeing constitutional protection for marriage equality.)

The competing principles, in this case, are irreconcilable; they are "in principle" opposed. What sort of process or engagement might Sandel—or anybody—suggest that might "finesse" this opposition, that might bring the opposing parties, if not into agreement, then into supportive tolerance of their opponents?

A genuine "communitarian" approach to this principled opposition on the issue of marriage equality must find some alternative to the typical "principle approach" to difference. Notice again that from our typical Platonist perspective, our only alternative is to accept and make evident the truth of one of the competing principles. The Biblical principle *or* the equality-under-the-law principle must be correct; both cannot be.

We must, perhaps through some subtlety of reason, be able to discern which is correct. Such is our duty in light of our Platonist heritage. And that heritage empowers not only our principled thought about such issues, but also the depth of conviction we feel that *our* side, *our* authority, is correct. Only some pathology of bigotry or prejudice or other irrational dimension of character, we feel, can account for the failure of our opponents to see what we know to be correct.

SANDEL'S SUGGESTION

When one moves beyond the Platonist, principled approach to such large social and divisive controversies as marriage equality, one is inevitably thrown onto realities of social life and their formative potentials. Families and communities of all kinds are foundations for individual character, and each such institution is constitutive, and may be more or less constructive in its contribution to our characters.

Sandel discerns that our relationships as citizens require that we think of ourselves as having a common life together, that we have in common specific ideals of national community, and that we share a common good *as citizens.* Sandel believes our commonality as citizens is vitally important to our cohesion as a national community. Whether we are Catholic or Protestant or Muslim or Mormon or Buddhist; whether we are rich or poor; whether we are white or black or Hispanic or Asian; whether we are recent arrivals as immigrants or descendents of generations of previous Americans; for all of these differences among us as citizens, we must find a way to cherish our common heritage and our common future. Our recent American history, unfortunately, pushes us away from that goal.

Politically and socially, what separates us from one another has become stronger than what unites us. We fail to understand how *those others* can be so obtuse, how what is so obvious to us they ignorantly fail to see.

We are Christians and those Muslims are against us. We are Muslims and those Christians do not understand us. We are Republicans and those liberals are against us. We are gay and in love with the man or woman we want to marry, and those conservative bigots have no consideration for our rights or feelings. We need the health care we have under Obamacare, and those Republicans want to take it away. We are young and healthy and don't want medical insurance and those Democrats are making us buy it anyway.

These divisions among Americans are reinforced by the segregation of news media into politically oriented segments that castigate political alternatives and opponents. The American community, *as* an American community, is disappearing. Our commonalities are becoming less important to us than our differences. And always: We are in the right, and those opposing us are pathological bigots.

These oppositional attitudes are remnants of our common Platonist heritage. Opposing views cannot both be true; our view derives from correct authority; and our opponent is defective or pathological in not seeing or acknowledging our authority and our truth. Sandel, however, does not succumb to this mistaken Platonist perspective. Sandel's communitarian perspective yields a constructive suggestion.

In Sandel's view, the most serious problem undermining the idea of all Americans as citizens of the same national community is wealth inequality. Here are Sandel's words:

> Too great a gap between rich and poor undermines the solidarity that democratic citizenship requires. Here's how: As inequality deepens, rich and poor live increasingly separate lives. The affluent send their children to private schools (or to public schools in wealthy suburbs), leaving urban public schools to the children of families who have no alternative. A similar trend leads to the secession by the privileged from other public institutions and facilities. Private health clubs replace municipal recreation centers and swimming pools. Upscale residential communities hire private security guards and rely less on public police protection. A second or third car removes the need to rely on public transportation. And so on. The affluent secede from public places and services, leaving them to those who can't afford anything else. (Sandel, Michael, *Justice: What's the Right Thing to Do?* 2009, 266)

The wealth gap undermines social solidarity among citizens of differing resources. Social divisions develop and become walls of misunderstanding. And added to stereotypes of race, religion, and sexual and gender preference, financial inequality among citizens undermines solidarity with other citizens. *The other* becomes a dangerous or feared dimension of our lives that we must subdue or eliminate, to the extent possible, from our daily lives. Again, Sandel's words:

> The hollowing out of the public realm makes it difficult to cultivate the solidarity and sense of community on which democratic citizenship depends. (Sandel 2009, 267)

"A Politics of Moral Engagement"

Sandel sees that without deliberate efforts to undermine our inertia toward social dissolution, we shall continue to dismember hopes for social solidarity. This solidarity among American citizens Alexis de Tocqueville noticed and remarked about extensively in his *Democracy in America* (See Tocqueville, Alexis de, *Democracy in America*, 2000). In the twenty-first century, as Sandel observes, that solidarity is under severe and increasing stress. Our deliberate efforts toward a new future solidarity must include a politics of moral engagement.

Sandel does not say a lot about what a politics of moral engagement looks like. The last page of his book is a suggestion that we might seek out ways of engaging different others (*the other*) in our American world so that we might better understand them and find ways to become, with them, an inclusive community sharing goals and ideals that unite us as citizens. To the extent that various communities and individuals have a common understanding of what a good life is, to that extent will they be able to agree about what justice is and what it means in specific contexts. How specifically we might achieve this end, Sandel leaves mostly to our imagination and creativity.

Since, however, this vague project seems our only hope to slow and maybe reverse the social and political dissolution of our American world, a world that is overwhelmingly "principled" and "Platonist," we must find ways to make that project concrete and determinate. The next chapter finds additional resources that can move us in that direction. Consider first, however, another prominent problem that has been with us throughout, the problem of justice among individuals and smaller communities.

Michael Brown and Darren Wilson Again

When Michael Brown and Darren Wilson come into the confrontation that results in Brown's death, all the variables of community and individuality that contribute to their understandings of the good come into play. In the current context, Brown and Wilson are *other* to each other. Although Brown and Wilson are not aware of differences in their understandings of a good life, their different understandings do come into play in their interaction. And not only their understandings of the good life, but also their understandings of their duties, their responsibilities and their privileges come into play in their interaction.

In the intensity of such interactions, every dimension of individual character comes into play. Different individuals in that same or a similar situation would yield a different sequence of events. Such situations of confrontation, of course, do elicit emotions and passions; however, the extent to which those dimensions of their characters dominate Brown and Wilson's interaction depends again upon the total content of their characters. How these elementary facts might help us understand what justice *is* in some way that is relevant to our concerns with racial justice is the crux of the matter. We must begin by seeing, as Sandel helps us to do, that the Platonist and principled approach to justice has intractable limitations.

And those limitations are not only structural limitations intent on the dissolution of our institutional social solidarity, as Sandel argues; they are also obstructions to interpersonal justice. If the black community in Ferguson had, as they did not, a sense of solidarity with their brothers serving as policemen in Ferguson, they would have had also an understanding of values and goods they had in common with their police brothers. And conversely, those policemen would have had a similar understanding of their commonality with their black brothers and sisters in the black community there.

Our American institutions, with their Platonist and Enlightenment roots, resist the solidarity Sandel and many others see that Americans need. Finding a way of thinking about ourselves, our institutions and communities that does not embody and encourage resistance to the solidarity we need, requires an alternative to those Platonist and Enlightenment roots.

We need, as Sandel sees, a politics of moral engagement. We need also a kind of interpersonal engagement that enables our seeing *the other* as individuals, as persons like ourselves and as fully deserving as are we. (Notice too that *the other* is as much a Platonist abstraction as are the *principles* discussed in previous chapters; it, as do they, holds others at a (convenient?) conceptual distance.)

CHAPTER 9

W.E.B. DuBois and John Dewey

Abstract Each of these thinkers—interestingly of the same generation—has an understanding of justice and the good that are indigenous to the American world and, more importantly, are not racist. This chapter explains the thought of DuBois and Dewey about these things and emphasizes their definitive differences from the conventional understandings of justice discussed in Part I. Both DuBois and Dewey seek an American democracy of brotherhood and sisterhood.

Keywords Democracy · Sympathy · Unity of virtues
Souls of Black Folk

W.E.B. DuBois and John Dewey are thinkers and philosophers of the same generation. DuBois lived from 1868 to 1963—95 years; Dewey lived from 1859 to 1952—92 years. Each man was a vital part of the intellectual culture of America throughout the first half of the twentieth century; each published widely in many popular venues, and each produced significant books taken seriously by the *cognoscenti* of their time. How can these men help us?

First, neither DuBois nor Dewey is a Platonist; both are aware of the dangers of Platonism and its intellectualizing of every dimension of life, along with its respect for authorities outside ourselves. In each of these men, respect for *reason*, either as an ultimate tool for finding truths about values (as in Plato) or as an alternative to other authorities

© The Author(s) 2018
S. Rosenbaum, *Race, Justice and American Intellectual Traditions*,
https://doi.org/10.1007/978-3-319-76198-5_9

(as in the Enlightenment), does not exist. Both DuBois and Dewey saw and argued for the subservience of reason to other dimensions of our humanity.

Second, both DuBois and Dewey were steeped from their earliest years in the central values of the American world. DuBois grew to maturity in Great Barrington, Massachusetts, where he internalized the values of freedom and equality, and aspired equally to the ideal of fraternity in a future American world. And Dewey came to maturity in Burlington, Vermont where he regularly attended the Congregational church as well as the town hall to participate in democratic processes of local governance. Their rural settings immersed each of these men in the cultures of democracy and Christianity. For those rural democratic and Christian cultural contexts, freedom and equality joined inextricably with fraternity. The unity of those values was an intimate part of DuBois and Dewey's common youthful world in that incubator of democracy that was New England in the middle of the nineteenth century.

Although both DuBois and Dewey felt in their hearts the vitality of their Christian, democratic values, neither was tempted toward the philosophical project of rationally certifying those values. Freedom, equality and fraternity lived vitally in their hearts, not primarily in their heads, and they lived their lives in light of and in defense of those values. Much can be said about their philosophical work and its avoidance of typical Western and Platonist tendencies of thought; however, for our purposes, we need note only their mutual resistance to Platonism and Enlightenment philosophy. Begin with DuBois.

W.E.B. DuBois

DuBois's *The Souls of Black Folk* (2007) is one of the best books of any genre of the twentieth century. DuBois's graceful style and his sensitivity to the plight of his fellow black Americans are unmatched in the literature of the twentieth century. Combined with these virtues, DuBois has a parallel sensitivity to the demand for intellectual rigor. And DuBois is as concerned with justice as is anybody in the American world. Here is what DuBois says about justice:

> Only by a union of intelligence and sympathy across the color-line in this critical period of the Republic shall justice and right triumph. (DuBois, W.E.B., *The Souls of Black Folk*, 2009, last sentence of Chapter 9)

In this remark, one sees immediately DuBois's concern with justice and how to achieve it. Justice comes only by a union of intelligence and sympathy across the color line. And although his concern here is with race, DuBois realizes that justice across any division comes only through a union of intelligence and sympathy.

The reason of Platonism or the rational principles of the Enlightenment do not figure into DuBois's account of how to achieve justice. Intelligence and sympathy are the keys. One might ask, how does intelligence differ from reason? Perhaps DuBois is suggesting simply that sympathy be added to the reason that was vital in the ancient world and in the Enlightenment?

No. Intelligence is different from reason. Reason is the faculty, in Plato and in the Enlightenment, that enables transcendence of the human world. Reason, in its very concept, enables bringing the transcendent into the human world and imposing it on behavior and practice. Platonist reason, as well as Enlightenment reason, in their intent, *coerce* behavior and practice. The authoritarian attitude embedded in deference to Aristotle ("The Philosopher") and in deference to The Church takes a different form in the Enlightenment and its respect for reason. DuBois, having studied with William James at Harvard, followed James in his resistance to imposing rational or Church authority on the human world.

In DuBois's work, what is human is precious and lovely, even in its basest condition, even in its least educated and least sophisticated condition. DuBois experienced and reported extensively about the hard lives of his black fellow Americans throughout the pages of *The Souls of Black Folk*. That book makes obvious DuBois's acute sensitivity to, and empathy with the plight of his black fellows. And nothing in DuBois's approach is rational or principled in the style of the thinkers in Part I. In DuBois's work, sympathy, empathy and intelligence do whatever constructive work is possible toward improving the human condition. And one should mark also that DuBois's depth of empathy for others was not limited to fellow black Americans; his extensive sensitivity to the human condition knew no racial limits. In *Souls*, for example, he remarks the plight of *all* southerners caught up in the maelstrom of The Civil War. (In his attitudes, DuBois is an American predecessor of Nelson Mandela.)

Chapter 2, "Of the Dawn of Freedom," exhibits DuBois's appreciation of the pathos of the Civil War and the plights of all those caught in it. Here is a passage.

Thus it is doubly difficult to write of this period calmly, so intense was the feeling, so mighty the human passions that swayed and blinded men. Amid it all, two figures ever stand to typify that day to coming ages,—the one, a gray-haired gentleman, whose fathers had quit themselves like men, whose sons lay in nameless graves; who bowed to the evil of slavery because its abolition threatened untold ill to all; who stood at last, in the evening of life, a blighted, ruined form, with hate in his eyes;—and the other, a form hovering dark and mother-like, her awful face black with the mists of centuries, had aforetime quailed at that white master's command, had bent in love over the cradles of his sons and daughters, and closed in death the sunken eyes of his wife,—aye, too, at his behest had laid herself low to his lust, and borne a tawny man-child to the world, only to see her dark boy's limbs scattered to the winds by midnight marauders riding after "cursed Niggers." These were the saddest sights of that woeful day; and no man clasped the hands of these two passing figures of the present-past; but, hating, they went to their long home, and, hating, their children's children live to-day.

Not only is DuBois attuned to the sufferings of black slaves; he is attuned also to the sufferings of the masters who are caught in the same social pathology as those slaves. No imposition of authority, rational or otherwise, might mitigate their suffering or the pathological social conditions that made it inevitable. DuBois is aware too of the *inertia* of those pathological social conditions: "... and, hating, their children's children live today." Our potential to escape those pathologies resides not in resort to reason. DuBois turns to intelligence and sympathy. Justice is possible only through the cooperation of intelligence and sympathy toward their common human goal.

DuBois, a century before him, understood the wisdom of Sandel's later achieved result. Neither reason, nor principle nor God can deliver us. Our responsibility is a human one, and is ours alone. We cannot hand off our responsibility to any authority. DuBois understood these things. And so too did John Dewey, DuBois's colleague in thought who was equally an intellectual giant of the twentieth century.

John Dewey

John Dewey's corpus of published work extends to thirty-seven volumes, not including his correspondence, and covering more than sixty years of American history. Dewey's talent for discursive thought is unparalleled in the modern world, and the breadth of his intellectual interest is equally extraordinary. (Dewey did produce a volume of poetry, but poetry turned out not to be his strength.)

Only one scholar (Robert Westbrook), to my knowledge, claims to have read Dewey's entire corpus, but fortunately reading its entirety is not a requirement of catching its spirit. Dewey, like DuBois, sees what reason cannot do. Dewey sees too why reason cannot do what centuries of Western intellectual culture hoped it would do. More specifically, when it comes to value issues, like justice, Dewey abandons entirely the goals and methods of Platonist and Enlightenment philosophy.

Dewey returns to the spirit of Solomon and to the community-oriented understanding of virtue many see rooted in Aristotle. Justice in Dewey's thought is not separable from other virtues. As in the story of Solomon, where his wisdom is inseparable from his just resolution of the women's argument over the child, so too in Dewey's thought wisdom and justice are inseparable.

Indeed, in Dewey as in Aristotle, virtue is one. Wisdom, courage, temperance and justice are separable only in thought about an occasion on which virtue appears. On one occasion, virtue appears as courage—as when one "speaks truth to power"; on another occasion, it appears as temperance—as when one "holds one's tongue"; on another, it appears as justice, as in the Biblical story. And wisdom is seeing the various situations that elicit virtuous behavior in proper perspective.

In Plato, these virtues are rooted in reason itself, and they have discreet, individual essences known only by the intellectually gifted. In Aristotle as in Dewey, the virtues are one and inseparable, but in Aristotle, and unlike Dewey, they are subject to the human *intellectual telos*. Neither the ancient philosophers nor their Enlightenment fellows acknowledge the *earthy* and *human* roots of all the virtues. Dewey acknowledges those roots.

Here are Dewey's words embracing the unity of the virtues, their inseparability other than in thought.

> The mere idea of a catalogue of different virtues commits us to the notion that virtues may be kept apart, pigeon-holed in water-tight compartments. In fact virtuous traits interpenetrate one another; this unity is involved in the very idea of integrity of character. At one time persistence and endurance in the face of obstacles is the most prominent feature; then the attitude is the excellence called courage. At another time, the trait of

impartiality and equity is uppermost, and we call it justice. At other times, the necessity for subordinating immediate satisfaction of a strong appetite or desire to a comprehensive good is the conspicuous feature. Then the disposition is denominated temperance, self-control. When the prominent phase is the need for thoughtfulness, for consecutive and persistent attention, in order that these other qualities may function, the interest receives the name of moral wisdom, insight, conscientiousness. In each case the difference is one of emphasis only.

This fact is of practical as well as theoretical import. The supposition that virtues are separated from one another leads, when it is acted upon, to that narrowing and hardening of action which induces many persons to conceive of all morality as negative and restrictive. (Dewey, John, *The Later Works, 1925–1953, Volume 7, Ethics*, 1985, 258)

To demand justice is to demand wisdom, temperance and courage. Virtue is one, and Dewey saw that our hunger for justice is inseparable from our hunger for freedom, equality and fraternity. Dewey saw, as did DuBois and later Sandel, that justice is inseparable from the good. Justice and goodness are, as are all virtues, embodied "together." Our understandings of those things must be united in order to avoid what Dewey calls "that narrowing and hardening of action" that leads to seeing morality as negative and restrictive. (For a more expansive account of how virtues are one in Dewey, see the chapter, "Ideals," in Rosenbaum, Stuart, *Pragmatism and the Reflective Life*, 2009.)

Dewey not only sees virtue as one; he sees also that democracy requires virtue. In democracy, as Dewey understood it and as it unfolded in his early life, freedom, equality and fraternity were "built in," as were the virtues. Dewey was "the philosopher of democracy," and as he understood democracy all citizens are, or are on their way toward becoming, virtuous. All citizens in a democracy are free and equal brothers.

As brothers, citizens of democracy respect and care for one another much as brothers do. Citizenship is as vital a relationship, in Dewey's thought, as is any community relationship. Religious congregations speak of one another as brothers and sisters. Labor unions speak of fellow members as brothers and sisters. So too, in Dewey's view, should citizens of a democracy. That "siblinghood" of citizens *is* democracy.

(In an early passage in Alexander McCall Smith's *Tears of the Giraffe*, 2009, Mma Ramotswe says to her American client, Andrea, "I will help you, my sister." Mma Ramotswe and Andrea exemplify the relationship Dewey sees as typical of citizens in a democracy.)

(And my British friend, Dee Blinka, once explained in a conversation about health-care policy that after the Second World War, all Britons knew that "every citizen counts." The British government, in consequence, implemented universal health care shortly after the war.)

Citizen relationships are the heart of democracy. Dewey sees that these relationships require not only tolerance of different others, but also the fraternity/sorority that hopes for, wants even to promote, their well-being. Here is a passage from a brief essay Dewey wrote in 1939 for the celebration of his eightieth birthday.

> Democracy is a way of life controlled by a working faith in the possibilities of human nature. Belief in the Common Man is a familiar article in the democratic creed. That belief is without basis and significance save as it means faith in the potentialities of human nature as that nature is exhibited in every human being irrespective of race, color, sex, birth and family, of material or cultural wealth. This faith may be enacted in statutes, but it is only on paper unless it is put in force in the attitudes which human beings display to one another in all the incidents and relations of daily life. To denounce Nazism for intolerance, cruelty and stimulation of hatred amounts to fostering insincerity if, in our personal relations to other persons, if, in our daily walk and conversation, we are moved by racial, color or other class prejudice; indeed, by anything save a generous belief in their possibilities as human beings, a belief which brings with it the need for providing conditions which will enable these capacities to reach fulfillment. The democratic faith in human equality is belief that every human being, independent of the quantity or range of his personal endowment, has the right to equal opportunity with every other person for development of whatever gifts he has. The democratic belief in the principle of leadership is a generous one. It is universal. It is belief in the capacity of every person to lead his own life free from coercion and imposition by others provided right conditions are supplied. (Dewey, John, "Creative Democracy, the Task Before Us," *The Collected Works of John Dewey*, 2008, paragraph 8)

This understanding of democracy is fulsome. This paragraph, indeed the entire essay, deserves serious and ongoing attention from every citizen of every aspiring democracy. (In fact, in my American philosophy class, I give extra credit to any student who is willing to memorize, and recite this paragraph on the last day of class.)

Dewey's words give substance to the cries of citizens for justice; his words show us what we can be as a democracy, what our lives might become as citizens who regard our fellows as brothers and sisters. We seek to realize not only our own hopes and aspirations, but also to provide, as we are able for the realization of the hopes and aspirations of fellow citizens.

DEMOCRACY

This idea of democracy is not simply the idea of freedom and autonomy writ political and social as it is in John Stuart Mill; nor is it the similar idea of freedom found in Milton Friedman that democracy is capitalist economic freedom inserted into every corner of our lives; nor is it even John Rawls's principles of justice seen as foundations for democracy. Sandel sees that none of these conceptual or ideological foundations captures our mutual understanding of democracy. Justice is inseparable from democracy; it is not a fixed, isolated or intellectually accessible idea independent of democracy. Ideological foundations do not yield the vitality of engagement that invests democracy with the loyalty of citizens. And democracy cannot survive without the loyalty of its citizens.

DuBois sees that justice needs intelligence and sympathy acting in concert. Dewey sees that democracy requires virtuous citizens and that justice is one with "other" virtues. These perspectives on democracy and justice cohere with Michael Sandel's conclusion that justice is inseparable from our understanding of the good. These perspectives concur that democratic citizenship includes, or should include justice in its very idea.

Citizenship must extend beyond one's own economic interests. One's economic interests are of course relevant; one must be able to satisfy basic needs. But for many individuals, economic interests are not the heart of their striving to realize themselves. A democratic world *enables* individuals, whether their interests are economic advance or artistic pursuit or otherwise.

In Dewey's thought, citizens believe in "the capacity of every person to lead his own life free from coercion and imposition by others provided right conditions are supplied." Part of our role as citizens is to let our fellows be themselves and to help them when they fall short of independent means ("right conditions") for achieving themselves. Dewey's resort to passive voice in this sentence should not deter us from appreciating the meaning or power of his claim.

We have responsibilities to our fellow citizens, not simply to leave them alone to pursue their own goals in whatever ways they can manage. Our fellow citizens *may not be able* to pursue their own goals without our help. Our responsibility as citizens is not only to tolerate our fellows; it is, in Dewey as in DuBois, to enable them to the extent we are able to do so. Fellow citizens are brothers and sisters.

CHAPTER 10

Some Contemporaries

Abstract Ta-Nehisi Coates, Bryan Stevenson and Michelle Alexander are some contemporary thinkers and activists who follow in the conceptual footsteps of DuBois and Dewey. This chapter considers each of those contemporaries and explains how each is a conceptual descendant of DuBois and Dewey. These contemporaries contribute distinctive ways of thinking about current issues of race in the American world, ways that follow the indigenous path blazed by DuBois and Dewey. The continuity in this indigenous American tradition of thought about justice is striking. Consequently, these contemporaries gain strength from realizing their continuity with those earlier—and pragmatist—traditions. This chapter concludes with comments about Coates's reflections about reparations as he presents them in his well-known *Atlantic* essay.

Keywords Samori · Walter McMillian · Josie · Criminals · Justice Poverty

The American world is steeped in racism. In spite of sincere self-inspection that does not find racism in our psyches, we nonetheless spontaneously say and do things that reveal it. Paula Ramsey Taylor, mentioned previously, is one example. Joe Wilson, the representative who yelled out "You lie" at President Obama's 2009 address on health care, is another. We should not be surprised at this basic fact about the American world.

© The Author(s) 2018
S. Rosenbaum, *Race, Justice and American Intellectual Traditions*,
https://doi.org/10.1007/978-3-319-76198-5_10

In previous chapters, we have seen how moral exemplars of the American world have revealed, unaware, their own racism. John Stuart Mill, Milton Friedman and John Rawls, among others, are examples of the racism embedded in American intellectual culture. We have seen, too, how they believed their intellectual commitments took them above the nitty-gritty of a racist social world filled with lynching and police shooting. But the cultural context that sustained their work is itself blind to its racism.

Platonism and the Enlightenment, with their dreams of bringing human reality to the heel of reason, feed at the same racist roots. Their justice, their morality is consistent with, and even embraces the human liability to xenophobia; it gerrymanders easily around structures of the social world like racism and homophobia. Reason, the heir of Platonism and the Enlightenment, has been able to achieve its goals only because of its isolation from the realities of the human world.

During the eighteenth and nineteenth centuries, reason gave humanity its rationale for the subservience of some to others, for white supremacy over black barbarians and slaves. (For an ambivalent perspective, see Joseph Conrad's *The Heart of Darkness*. And remember that Conrad's work, unlike Mill's, is literature and thus is less amenable to rational gerrymandering of social reality than is the discursion of Mill, Friedman or Rawls.) After DuBois and Dewey, social reality must be met on its own terms, not brought to heel by discursive rationality. Some important contemporaries exemplify this social realism and seek to invest it with the spirit of democracy that lives in the thought of those American thinkers.

Bryan Stevenson, Ta-Nehisi Coates, Michelle Alexander

These three individuals are early twentieth-century shadows of W.E.B. DuBois. They are perceptive observers of the American cultural scene, especially as regards the issue of racism. All write gripping narrative accounts, both concrete and general, of the racism pervading American culture. All are aware of the self-deception in the ubiquitous naïve belief that we can inspect our own psyches to discover whether or not we are racists. If I were able to compile a list of books that all Americans must read, the books of these three would top the list.

Bryan Stevenson

Just Mercy (2014) is the intriguing title of Bryan Stevenson's book that has an equally intriguing subtitle, *A Story of Justice and Redemption*. The story of justice and redemption Stevenson tells is mainly about his client, Walter McMillian.

Monroe County, Alabama wrongly convicted McMillian of murder. McMillian's conviction was not just a mistake; it was an egregious, intentional injustice plotted and committed against an innocent man. McMillian was black and vulnerable. The story Stevenson tells about McMillian's conviction is compelling and poignant. The concreteness of detail Stevenson gives resonates with the same detail DuBois gives in *The Souls of Black Folk*. Just as DuBois gives readers the real people he writes about, so too does Stevenson. (As we remember Josie from DuBois's *Souls*, so we remember Walter from Stevenson's *Just Mercy*.) Lives and their vicissitudes and hardships live in each sentence these authors write. Walter McMillian served six years on death row for a murder he did not commit, and the evidence of his innocence was obvious even to cursory inspection. Stevenson, however, had to work long, intense hours over many years to secure McMillian's release. How do these travesties of "justice" happen?

Stevenson gives enough detail in McMillian's case to enable a clear explanation of how the travesty happened to him. The short answer is racism. And of course, also the poverty of a life lived at the edge of society, a life that took what satisfactions it might find in family, church and community in spite of its poverty. Walter's is not the only case Stevenson mentions, but Walter's is the case woven throughout his narrative of injustice.

The injustices Stevenson shows us are palpable. Nobody can remain unmoved by those injustices. Stevenson also tells us what injustice is, and he does so in a way that could follow only on the intellectual context provided by DuBois and Dewey. The *reason* of our Platonist heritage and of the Enlightenment—along with the racism that goes with it—fades into an archaic background. Here are Stevenson's words.

> My work with the poor and the incarcerated has persuaded me that the opposite of poverty is not wealth; the opposite of poverty is justice. Finally, I've come to believe that the true measure of our commitment to justice, the character of our society, our commitment to the rule of law, fairness, and equality cannot be measured by how we treat the rich, the powerful,

the privileged, and the respected among us. The true measure of our character is how we treat the poor, the disfavored, the accused, the incarcerated, and the condemned. (18)

Notice Stevenson's semantic innovation: *The opposite of poverty is justice.* Sounds oxymoronic. Justice we think opposes injustice; poverty we think opposes wealth. Stevenson is correcting our conventional presumption, and he is doing it in a way consistent with DuBois and Dewey's suggestions.

DuBois tells us that only sympathy united with intelligence can yield justice. Dewey tells us that justice is not separable from the other virtues, in particular from sympathy and love. Stevenson's innovation follows in the path trod by those earlier American thinkers. What we must do is to cease crying out for justice *in itself,* justice in its purity and isolation from our understanding of the good or from our understanding of sympathy, mercy and love. (*Just Mercy* is Stevenson's title.)

Justice requires our recognition that fellow citizens, despite their color or ethnic background, are our brothers and sisters. And as Stevenson also says, just before the above quotation, "*Each of us is more than the worst thing we've ever done.*" (18) Each of us knows this simple truth about our biological brothers and sisters, as do our parents about each of us. Justice requires our recognition that this simple truth covers also our *citizen* brothers and sisters.

Justice and good are inseparable. Justice and sympathy are inseparable. Justice and love are inseparable. These truths are available to us once we see beyond our Platonist and Enlightenment intellectual heritage. Also available to us are our failures to see one another as the brothers and sisters we know in our hearts we are. These failures of vision are the subjects of Ta-Nihisi Coates and Michelle Alexander.

TA-NIHISI COATES AND MICHELLE ALEXANDER

Ta-Nihisi Coates writes in a powerfully poignant way about the psychological realities our black brothers and sisters face. Michelle Alexander writes in a powerfully poignant way about the social and political realities our black brothers and sisters face.

Coates writes in the form of a letter to his son, Samori, about the uncertain world their living must accommodate. Coates and Samori's world is, as is the world of each of us, set in history, community and family; their psyches are, as are ours, set in history, community and family.

The plunder of black life was drilled into this country in its infancy and reinforced across its history, so that plunder has become an heirloom, an intelligence, a sentience, a default setting to which, likely to the end of our days, we must invariably return. (Coates, Ta-Nehisi, *Between the World and Me*, 2015, 111)

The pervasiveness of racism in American history and society has become a fixture in black psyches—indeed in all of our psyches. Coates knows that his son must live within his own roots in an historical, social world not of his choosing. Coates knows as well that Samori must live in the meager promise of a social world that is as terrible as it is beautiful. The beauty of our hopes and ideals must always negotiate with the terror of a real social and historical world.

Coates quotes Solzhenitsyn, "To do evil a human being must first of all believe that what he's doing is good, or else that it's a well-considered act in conformity with natural law." Coates continues,

This is the foundation of the Dream—its adherents must not just believe in it but believe that it is just, believe that their possession of the Dream is the natural result of grit, honor, and good works. There is some passing acknowledgement of the bad old days, which, by the way, were not so bad as to have any ongoing effect on our present. (Coates, 98)

Coates sees that the evil men do, they do not recognize as evil. (Plato made this same observation, I think in *Meno*.) And we all believe that we live mostly in the light of truth and justice; our own psyches exempt us from evil doing. Just as we do not see racism when we look within, we also see purity within ourselves when we inspect our motives and actions. We sometimes acknowledge that when we are angry or depressed or under some baleful influence we "are not ourselves" and may stoop to less than our customary nobility. What we usually fail to acknowledge are our historical and social heritages and their contributions to who we are.

Our psyches are not "blank slates" from which we build characters through our own "grit, honor, and good works." We have inheritances. These inheritances partly, perhaps largely, constitute our psyches. John Dewey too recognizes this fact and makes it central to his moral thought. Here is how Dewey puts the same point in his 1908 *Ethics*, written with James H. Tufts:

A man's power is due (1) to physical heredity; (2) to social heredity ... (3) to his own efforts. Individualism may properly claim this third factor. It is just to treat men unequally so far as their efforts are unequal. It is socially desirable to give as much incentive as possible to the full development of everyone's powers. But this very same reason demands that in the first two respects we treat men as equally as possible. (Quoted in Peter Manicas, "John Dewey and the Problem of Justice," 1981, 8.)

Dewey and Coates recognize that our very psyches, the very selves we are and believe and act from, are not simply *ours*. Our psyches are historical, social and familial as well as biological.

We have no control over our biological inheritance; we have no control over our social inheritance. These biological and social factors augment or diminish our prospects for success in our lives. Our "grit" contributes little on its own to our prospects.

The "justice" we naively believe is to be meted out objectively and dispassionately and has a content of its own apart from biology, society and history is a Platonist and Enlightenment construct it is an ideological residue that hangs on in our social worlds. Coates understands this simple truth, as do Stevenson, Dewey and DuBois. Bringing this simple truth into play in our real worlds means acknowledging the unity among justice, wisdom, temperance and courage; it means acknowledging as well the inseparability of justice from ideas of the good; and acknowledging as well that justice is the product of intelligence and sympathy; and acknowledging, with Stevenson, that justice and mercy are one.

Michelle Alexander too recognizes the wisdom in Coates, Stevenson, Dewey and DuBois's approach to justice. Alexander's *The New Jim Crow* expresses acute awareness of the various forms racism has taken throughout American history. And in the contemporary world, a cleverly disguised racism takes the form of an imposed criminality. Recall the quotation from Chapter 4 above:

Arguably the most important parallel between mass incarceration and Jim Crow is that both have served to define the meaning and significance of race in America. Indeed, a primary function of any racial caste system is to define the meaning of race in its time. Slavery defined what it meant to be black (a slave), and Jim Crow defined what it meant to be black (a second-class citizen). Today mass incarceration defines the meaning of blackness in America: black people, especially black men, are criminals. That is what it means to be black. (Alexander, Michelle, *The New Jim Crow*, 2010, 197)

Alexander sees and makes an elaborate case that the war on drugs is indeed an updated technique for keeping black people and white people in, respectively, inferior and superior social positions. The racist economy of slavery is replicated in Jim Crow laws and is further replicated in the war on drugs. Our visceral reaction to drug use is a convenient mask for our visceral reaction to the black *other*. Indeed that visceral racism first gave life to and continues to nourish the visceral reaction to drug use.

Alexander explains in detail how drug law and its enforcement are effective tools for keeping in place the structures of racial inequality pervasive in the American world. Alexander also sees, and reiterates throughout her book, that responsibility for the racism that persists throughout American culture is *not* the criminality of black men and women, but the natural inferiority of their characters and communities. Alexander sees that the responsibility for that racism—and the criminality white Americans see in it—belongs to all Americans. All citizens are brothers and sisters. Alexander quotes W.E.B. DuBois as follows,

> The burden belongs to the nation, and the hands of none of us are clean if we bend not our energies to righting these great wrongs. (Alexander 2010, 217)

Alexander sees, with DuBois and Dewey and Sandel that black Americans are, unlike the black *other* (the abstraction that conveniently hides from us our own racism), fellow citizens who happen to be black and descendents of former slaves. Fellow citizens are, in Sandel, Dewey and DuBois, our brothers and sisters. We owe our fellow citizens more than simply not enslaving them or not discriminating against them as they seek to exercise their rights as citizens. The Freedom, autonomy and equality rooted in our Constitution and in Enlightenment intellectual culture are, as these thinkers recognize, inadequate to our democracy.

We owe fellow citizens two things. (1) We owe the bond of fraternity/sorority that seeks to enable, in the ways we can do so, their efforts to realize themselves. (2) We owe also our acknowledgement of the American history to which we are all heirs that is thoroughly and deeply racist. Ta-Nihisi Coates focuses in an essay for *The Atlantic* on item (2), our responsibility to acknowledge our racist American history and the role of *all* Americans in that history.

REPARATIONS

Coates's essay in *The Atlantic* is "The Case for Reparations." (2014) Reparations proposals address item (2) above, our responsibility to acknowledge our racist roots.

Reparations to former slaves and their descendents is an issue that frequently, if not usually, draws a scornful response. (A delightful essay in *The American Scholar* in 2007 exemplifies this typical response, but without the customary scornful tone. See Beauchamp, Gorman, "Apologies All Around," 2007.) Coates, however, believes that without acknowledgement of our slave-holding and racist past, along with the ways that past has permeated our contemporary lives, Americans will be unable to progress toward the justice our contemporary world needs. Coates knows, as well, that the prospects for reparations are at best slight.

Coates would have us begin with HR 40. John Conyers, a Michigan representative, introduced HR 40 in 1989 and has reintroduced it in each successive legislative term. The resolution would establish a Commission to Study Reparation Proposals for African Americans. The resolution has never been debated and has never come to a vote. HR 40 is, as some would say, a "non-starter." Political realities are political realities. Coates is nevertheless insistent.

The brutalities inflicted on black Americans for 250 years of slavery and another 150 years of racist policy and practice, in Coates's view, merit at least public conversation about those years of slavery and racism. Coates insists that Americans must at least acknowledge that their glorious history, and even their ideal of democracy, rest on a foundation of brutality and immorality. Our American integrity requires acknowledging our sordid past. (A small analogy appears in the contemporary German culture that is laced with reminders of the horrors of a Nazi regime that wrought a campaign of genocide against their Jewish brothers and sisters.) Here are Coates's words.

> And so we must imagine a new country. Reparations—by which I mean the full acceptance of our collective biography and its consequences—is the price we must pay to see ourselves squarely .... Reparations beckon us to reject the intoxication of hubris and see America as it is—the work of fallible humans. (Coates, Ta-Nehisi, *The Atlantic*, 2014, 54)

And again,

> What I'm talking about is more than recompense for past injustices—more than a handout, a payoff, hush money, or a reluctant bribe. What I'm talking about is a national reckoning that would lead to spiritual renewal. Reparations would mean the end of scarfing hot dogs on the fourth of July while denying the facts of our heritage. Reparations would mean the end of yelling "patriotism" while waving a Confederate flag. Reparations would mean a revolution of the American consciousness, a reconciling of our self-image as the great democratizer with the facts of our history. (Coates, *The Atlantic*, 54)

Coates is persuasive, both in this powerful essay championing reparations and in his book-length letter to his son, Samori. Coates sees, in the same way DuBois and Dewey saw, that democracy and justice must be more tightly woven together than our Enlightenment intellectual inheritance enables. As Coates puts it, "we must imagine a new country." The justice required for a successful democracy, a successful America, must transcend its Enlightenment foundations.

John Stuart Mill, Milton Friedman, and even John Rawls cannot supply the intellectual foundations for a successful democratic world. The world of American society and politics must find a way to rise above its Constitution—and the Enlightenment ideological constraints that Constitution imposes. Our own American intellectual heroes—DuBois and Dewey—show us the way to imagining a new country.

Recall the two things we owe fellow citizens mentioned above: (1) the bond of fraternity/sorority that seeks to enable, in the ways we can do so, their efforts to realize themselves and (2) our acknowledgement of the American history that includes 400 years of slavery and racism. Coates is right that the new country we must imagine requires looking squarely at the American history and culture that emerged from our pervasive commitments to genocide, slavery and racism. Our meeting that responsibility, however, is only half of what we need to do. The other half is finding ways to encourage in ourselves and in our fellow citizens recognition of the bonds of citizenship, the bonds of "siblinghood" that hold us in a national *community* and enable us to respect one another and to work toward common goals.

CHAPTER 11

Our Future

Abstract This chapter concludes by offering a specific diagnosis of contemporary American conundrums about race as well as specific constructive suggestions for addressing those conundrums. Paul Krugman, David Brooks and Sheryl Cashin are prominent characters in the discussion of this last chapter. The suggestions require us to move beyond fundamentalist, Enlightenment ideologies of society and politics and to embrace fully the indigenous intellectual traditions of our American world. These indigenous traditions enable a move beyond ideological opposition into a brotherhood and sisterhood of citizenship.

Keywords Politics of principle · Politics of sympathy
Politics of fairness

American culture is a hodgepodge of diverse intellectual commitments. Many of these commitments find reinforcement in news and social media venues, and frequently they correspond loosely with some political orientation.

The strictly Constitutional, and Enlightenment, orientation— "liberalism" in John Stuart Mill and Milton Friedman—finds its strongest political advocates in the Republican Party. For these strict constitutionalist individuals, the whole of any citizen's responsibility to any other citizen is to leave them alone, to leave them free to pursue their own goals in any way they might wish, within the limits of the law.

© The Author(s) 2018
S. Rosenbaum, *Race, Justice and American Intellectual Traditions*,
https://doi.org/10.1007/978-3-319-76198-5_11

These individuals value the freedom and autonomy guaranteed in the American Constitution above all else, along with personal virtues that complement those values.

Self-reliance and independence are personal virtues that complement freedom and autonomy. The equality guaranteed in our Constitution, however, these "liberal" individuals see as subservient to the freedom and autonomy they cherish. Unlike these "liberals," other Americans take the equality commitment of our Constitution more seriously. (I put "liberal" in scare quotes here because it has become a term of derision among those same Republicans who see themselves as conservatives.)

These other Americans who take the value of equality more seriously believe that the principles of justice John Rawls offers are more appropriate to the realities of our American world. Rawls's two principles do raise equality to parity with freedom and autonomy. Those principles of justice, however, lack the deep roots of the Constitutional values of freedom and autonomy. And Republican Party values in the contemporary world remain deeply rooted in the Enlightenment. (Republicans might have studied social or political philosophy and thereby encountered Rawls's work on justice; if they did so, they likely noticed the controversy about the rationality of choices made from "the original position," and may have discounted Rawls for that reason.)

Our Republican conservatives believe, along with Mill and Friedman, that individual freedom and autonomy are the most important values of American democracy. Republican respect for those liberal values has become linked by political expediency with the traditional social and moral values that defined America in the nineteenth and early twentieth centuries. Women's subservience to men; marriage between one man and one woman; separation of the races socially and maritally; the reprehensibility of homosexuality; and moral opposition to drug use; these values Republicans have embraced as a way of affirming their traditional value orientation and expanding their political appeal.

Traditional values Republicans embrace thus include the freedom and autonomy written into our Constitution, along with the social and moral values of the nineteenth and early twentieth centuries. Equality as an Enlightenment value equal to freedom and autonomy, Republicans see is not written *originally* into our Constitution, and they see as well the political expediency of embracing traditional values and the racism that goes with those values. Equality gets short shrift in the contemporary political world, as least as far as Republican politics is concerned.

My suggestion is that Republicans are, at least mostly, men and women of principle. Republican values are the values our founding fathers wrote into our Constitution and defended by prominent Enlightenment thinkers—in this book by John Stuart Mill and Milton Friedman. Consider the following exchange between a television journalist and a Republican congressman.

> *Reporter*: "Do you believe every American has a basic right to health care?"
> *Congressman*: "I think Americans have the right to life, liberty and the pursuit of happiness."

One might see this exchange as simply evasive in the style of political exchange. But one might see the exchange also as the congressman's resolute expression of principle. Our Constitution guarantees Americans rights to life, liberty and the pursuit of happiness; our Constitutional guarantees extend no further, and especially they do not extend to guarantees of health care.

Paul Ryan, the Speaker of the House of Representatives in 2017, explicitly embraces this Enlightenment, Constitutional perspective and reportedly suggests that his staff read Ayn Rand's *Atlas Shrugged*; Rand is a prominent liberal/libertarian thinker of the twentieth century. Ryan's commitment to freedom and autonomy as the most basic values of American democracy is legendary. As is too Ryan's desire to eliminate Medicaid and Medicare as federal programs.

This fundamental and principled commitment to Enlightenment and Constitutional social and political philosophy is characteristic of Republican politicians in the contemporary American world. How else are we to make sense of their political commitments? Paul Krugman, a columnist for the *New York Times* and a professor of economics at Princeton University seems not to acknowledge the *principled* character of Republican political positions.

PAUL KRUGMAN

In a column titled, "Understanding Republican Cruelty," Krugman seeks to explain the cruelty of Republican health-care legislation.

The puzzle—and it is a puzzle, even for those who have long since concluded that something is terribly wrong with the modern G.O.P.—is why the party is pushing this harsh, morally indefensible agenda... .. So it's vast suffering ... imposed on many of our fellow citizens in order to give a handful of wealthy people what amounts to some extra pocket change... .. Which brings me back to my question: Why would anyone want to do this? (Krugman, Paul, *New York Times,* June 30, 2017)

The morally indefensible agenda Krugman is trying to explain is the legislative proposal that takes Medicaid away from 22 million low-income Americans, while giving a tax break to the wealthiest 2% of Americans. Krugman sees this legislation as cruelty, as do most Americans who become aware of its content, including especially its democratic opponents. Krugman explains this Republican cruelty by "a politically convenient lie,"

> [T]he pretense, going all the way back to Ronald Reagan, that social safety net programs just reward lazy people who don't want to work. And we all know which people in particular were supposed to be on the take. (Krugman 2017)

The people "on the take" in Reagan's opposition to welfare were black Americans. In the political idiom of Reagan's time, those black Americans were "welfare queens driving Cadillacs." In Krugman's account,

> [T]he modern G.O.P. basically consists of career apparatchiks who live in an intellectual bubble, and those Reagan-era stereotypes still dominate their picture of struggling Americans. (Krugman 2017)

Krugman's explanation of Republican cruelty is Republican reliance on stereotypes from a bygone era, along with their own and their supporter's racism.

I confess sympathy with Krugman's perspective. However, I believe it does not quite do justice to Republicans as an explanation of their typical political proposals. Paul Ryan, for example, is quite explicit about his commitment to Constitutional ideals of freedom and autonomy.

Ryan is an intellectual descendent of John Stuart Mill, Milton Friedman and Ayn Rand; he is an idealist committed to the Enlightenment values expressed most vigorously in those thinkers. Constitutional idealist, yes, Ryan is that. But perhaps too Ryan is an American, Enlightenment ideologue?

The Politics of Principle

Paul Ryan is a typical Republican politician. Ryan is rhetorically talented and photogenic. Ryan, too, like all of us, has his own experience, along with the cultural, familial and religious backgrounds that yield his identity. Somewhere along his way, Ryan drank deeply from the well of Enlightenment individualism that included its twentieth-century intellectual representatives. In some minds, presumably including Ryan's, those draughts are intoxicating and life-shaping. In consequence, Ryan became the Republican politician he is today. Of course, being a man of principle as I suggest Ryan is, means in our American political world being clever enough to gerrymander one's commitments publicly so that they become palatable to a majority of relevant voters. The main tool in the Republican arsenal for such clever gerrymandering is a commitment to conservative, traditional "family values." Paul Ryan's politics is a composite of liberal (Enlightenment) principle and traditional American values. Politicians of that sort are, in our contemporary American world, known as conservatives.

What Paul Krugman misses in the stance of typical Republican politicians on issues like health care is the *principle* in their stance. The politicians Krugman does not understand seek to move toward the ideal of an individualistic world captured in Enlightenment political philosophy and in our American Constitution. *Republicans are utopians*. And Republicans see politics as the art of sidling gradually toward an ideal—and Enlightenment—society. Why should we not join in their pursuit of an ideal Enlightenment world? Two answers to this question offer themselves.

The first and short answer is that those Republican politicians are fundamentalist ideologues. ("Fundamentalist" and "ideologue" are ugly words, but they are descriptive.) Another part of that same answer is that, like John Stuart Mill and Milton Friedman, they are racists.

"I Am Not a Racist"

Part of Enlightenment individualism is the myth that individuals *know* themselves, that individuals are consciously aware of their own values and beliefs. In an Enlightenment intellectual world, individuals are *transparent* to themselves; they can *see* who and what they are. In that world, "looking inside oneself" reveals who and what one is. Recall Paula Ramsey Taylor's response to the suggestion that her tweet about Michelle Obama was racist. Ms. Taylor knew—because she knew herself—that she was not a racist, as she explained in a later tweet.

Enlightenment philosophers saw themselves as seeking what reason required, and they had the confidence that if they found it, they could of course do or believe accordingly. About the transparency of their psyches to themselves, they had no doubt. An exception is the notorious skeptic, David Hume (1711–1776).

Hume's skeptical argument against a soul or self we can know by "looking inside" is that when he looks inside himself he sees *nothing like a self*; he sees only an ongoing sequence of passing experiences. (See Hume, David, *Treatise on Human Nature*, 1960, 1.4.6.3.)

David Hume was the premier skeptic of the Enlightenment and Hume knew at least that individuals are *not* transparent to themselves and that they cannot simply *see* who or what they are. Part of Republican and Enlightenment ideology is not just the freedom and autonomy written into our American Constitution, but also the idea that we can know ourselves simply by "looking inside." When we do "look inside," however, we miss a bunch of ugliness, including our racism. (And the nineteenth and twentieth-century post-Enlightenment thinkers who enabled the realization that we are not transparent to ourselves, most prominently Charles Darwin and Sigmund Freud, had not yet appeared on the European scene.)

Racism and the politics of principle are inseparable. Not only principle, but also racism is prevalent in the world of contemporary American Republican politics. Histories of this connection are fairly easy to trace. (For a simple example, see Rosenbaum, Stuart, *Recovering Integrity*, 2015, 1–3.) Our deep affection for the individualism of Enlightenment philosophy carries with it an associated affection for racism, along with an affection for the myth that we can know ourselves simply by "looking inside."

(An interesting historical question is why and how contemporary European culture has mostly avoided the Enlightenment's principled individualism and its associated racism that is so prevalent in the American world. Much speculation is possible here, but it should probably include the entanglements of European social fabrics with some of the most destructive wars of human history during the twentieth century. Recall, for example, the comment of my British friend, Dee Blinka, about the universal health care instituted in Britain after World War Two mentioned in Chapter 9.)

ANOTHER ANSWER

Recall the question above about why we should not join our Republican brothers in hewing to the Enlightenment and Constitutional values written into America's founding documents. The short answer above was that those Republican brothers are fundamentalist ideologues. This answer might be elaborated further, but another answer offers itself and is supported by the work of Michael Sandel, W.E.B. DuBois and John Dewey. Sandel, DuBois and Dewey see the clay feet of the Enlightenment and it's political, social and moral thought; they see that the Enlightenment emperor written into our Constitution has no clothes. More directly, those thinkers see that the contemporary world has no need for the Enlightenment's fundamentalist ideology.

Perhaps of interest also is that these thinkers have no sympathy either with fundamentalist *religious* ideology. DuBois was a student of William James who saw, likely because of his early work in psychology, the ideological fervor/fever of Enlightenment philosophers. James, of course, was a pragmatist. And John Dewey too was a pragmatist and the most important philosopher of twentieth-century America. Ideology, along with foundational rational principle, those thinkers saw as archaic remainders of Western European intellectual culture. Much to say, of course, about pragmatism and its vicissitudes in the American world, but primary to pragmatism is its opposition to ideological rigidity, its opposition to official Western orthodoxies of all kinds. Each of these thinkers, along with those addressed in the previous chapter, strikes out in a new direction that coheres more readily with social and political realities of the contemporary American world.

POLITICS OF SYMPATHY

An alternative to the politics of principle finds life in the thought of those classical American thinkers, some historical and some contemporary, mentioned previously in Part II.

Sandel's suggestion that justice has no life apart from some idea of the good reflects the need to transcend ideological principle. Likewise, DuBois and Dewey—pragmatists in their hearts—live from their hearts rather than their heads. Bryan Stevenson, Ta-Nehisi Coates and Michelle Alexander live also from their hearts rather than from their heads. Our need to address critical problems of our American world requires not rationally defensible principles we are committed to applying come what may, but empathetic concern for the plights of fellow Americans.

In the view of all these thinkers, we can address constructively the concrete realities our fellow citizens face only by policies deliberately designed to address *those* realities. If our fellow citizens have no social support structures that enable their participation *as* citizens, we must provide such structures. Food, jobs, education, health care—these we know are basic to personal success in our world. We must see these things into the hands of fellow citizens who need them.

But—our *principled* reaction—our country was founded on the values of freedom and autonomy, along with the principled commitment to guaranteeing *those* things to fellow citizens. Yes, those are our founding values. In the contemporary world, however, equality of opportunity has become a pressing need, especially in those parts of the American world where it is missing. We do know that the *intent* of our Constitution, *as amplified by its amendments*, is to guarantee equality as well as freedom and autonomy to all citizens.

Our Constitutional mandate for equality, along with freedom and autonomy, requires a politics of sympathy. Acknowledging equality with our fellow citizens requires sympathy. Again as DuBois puts it, "only by a union of intelligence and sympathy … can justice be achieved." And as Dewey puts the point in "Creative Democracy" and in his *Ethics*, justice, sympathy and love yield a harmony that justice "itself"—that creature of principle— cannot achieve. And in Stevenson's terms, "the opposite of poverty is justice."

The freedom, autonomy and equality guaranteed by our Constitution to all citizens will not arrive through principled adherence to an archaic ideology. We must abandon social and political ideologies and turn toward our humanity, toward our hearts rather than our heads. How might we make this turn?

Constructive Suggestions

What I called above a politics of sympathy, Sheryll Cashin calls a politics of fairness. (See Cashin, Sheryll, *Place not Race*, 2014.) Here are her words.

> What we need is a politics of fairness, one in which people of color and the white people who are open to them move past racial resentment to form an alliance of the sane. The sanity alliance might get some things done for the common good of all of us. (110)

Cashin also believes we might constructively cease trying for affirmative action by racial category and to move instead to affirmative action by social category. Underprivileged white citizens are just as *underprivileged* as underprivileged black citizens. Our primary problem, Cashin believes, is the inertia of privilege in the American world, and that inertia excludes not just *racial* minorities.

I believe Cashin intends the same idea I see deriving from DuBois and Dewey, Stevenson, Coates and Alexander. Her suggestion too is an effort to undermine the politics of principle, along with the unacknowledged racism that constrains our ability to address the inertia of privilege. A politics of sympathy, I believe, comports more easily with the idea that fellow citizens, simply *as* citizens, deserve our respect and help. Citizens are brothers and sisters with whom we sympathize even if we cannot always lighten their load. (Cashin's use of *fairness* as an alternative to *principle* seems to me insufficiently distinct in its rhetorical appeal; it echoes too loudly Rawls's thought about justice.)

As fellow citizens, however, we must sympathize with and hope for and argue for our colleague citizens' access to means of realizing themselves—at least in the most basic ways we ourselves enjoy. Our political, social problem is finding ways to move from principle to sympathy, from head to heart, from *the other* to others.

DAVID BROOKS'S BILLION DOLLARS

David Brooks, too, sees the need for a politics of sympathy rather than our customary politics of principle. In a column for the *New York Times* titled "Giving Away Your Billion," Brooks imagines what he would do with a hypothetical billion dollars he could give away to any cause he wanted (Brooks, David, *New York Times*, June 6, 2017). The point of Brooks's proposal is to enable our understanding of socially and economically different others.

> What would I do if I had a billion bucks to use for good? I'd start with the premise that the most important task before us is to reweave the social fabric. People in disorganized neighborhoods need to grow up enmeshed in the loving relationships that will help them rise. The elites need to be reintegrated with their own countrymen.
>
> Only loving relationships transform lives, and such relationships can be formed only in small groups. Thus, I'd use my imaginary billion to seed 25-person collectives around the country. (Brooks, David, *New York Times*, June 6, 2017)

In Brooks's idea, the 25 person collectives would deliberately cross soci-oeconomic divides in order to create "a baseline of sympathy and under-standing." Brooks's small collectives would be lifelong support groups, extended families that work in much the way extended biological families work. Such collectives would be mixed socially, economically and racially, and they would be *funded* to enable regular meetings and in order to deal with occasional crises their members might encounter. The collec-tives would be social foci for their members. As "families," the collectives would function much like families, though their diversity would enable sympathy and understanding across a wide diversity of social, economic and racial categories.

In Brooks's imagined spending of his billion, the collectives would "hit the four pressure points required for personal transformation": heart—nurturing deep friendships; hands—performing small tasks of ser-vice for one another; head—reading to nourish intellectual virtues; and soul—discussing fundamental issues of life's purpose.

In a social and political world of entrenched and principled division, Brooks's billion spent in the way he imagines would be a constructive contribution to the American world. Something must be done to over-come our ever more deeply engrained social, economic and racial divi-sions. A politics of sympathy needs a foundation in social and political reality, and in the American world, only an idealistic benefactor might engineer its fundamentals. Our dominant politics of principle means no public source of funding is possible. Brooks, unfortunately, lacks the bil-lion needed to put in place his scheme. That such a scheme would work its weal, however, is clear.

The key to sympathy is understanding and personal relationship. These things are available to any one of us in relation to any others among us. Recall Bryan Stevenson's first visit to his death row client in Alabama.

Stevenson was nervous and had no idea how his one-hour appoint-ment with Henry on Georgia's death row might go. To Stevenson's surprise, his one-hour appointment turned into a three-hour congenial conversation with Henry, the prisoner who was delighted with the news that he would not be executed within the next year. The stereotypes that had dominated Stevenson's thought about death row inmates dissolved in the immediacy of relationship that developed in his conversation with Henry. Sympathy requires relationship.

A recent, perhaps odd-seeming indicator of this fact is research show-ing that we might be able to "fall in love with anybody." Mandy Lee Catron wrote an essay describing her experience of getting into love deliberately, by chosen actions that led to her being in love. Ms. Catron did not "fall in love"; rather she chose to be in love with a specific man she suspected *might* be right for her. She followed the prescription of psychologist Arthur Aron, who saw two strangers fall in love in his laboratory.

The key to achieving the desired result was enabling two people to become vulnerable to one another, to sympathize with and to under-stand one another. Aron set a series of thirty-six question two individuals would answer for each other over a period of ninety minutes, after which time, they would look into one another's eyes for four minutes. Whether or not Aron's procedure is "scientifically reliable," it does illustrate that sympathy and vulnerability are keys to understanding and appreciating others. Aron's experiment had the explicit design of achieving that result. And at least in some cases, it worked.

All these Part II thinkers do or would acknowledge that sympathy yields a result different from principle. Principle sees others as *the other*, a fixed stereotype needing rules to control how *it* impinges on our lives. The politics of principle is the art of finding constitutional ways of con-trolling *the other* and limiting *its* effect on us.

Others are not fixed stereotypes. Others are people like us, different in many ways, but sharing a humanity that enables us to sympathize with their plights. (*The other* does not have plights! Or feelings!) Our hope for the American world is finding ways to escape the politics of principle and move toward the politics of sympathy.

Another part of our hope is more difficult. The more difficult part is finding our way out of the conceptual clutches of the Enlightenment and embracing those American thinkers whose thought is more congenial to our needs for sympathy and fraternity. Addressing this more difficult part is a topic for another time and also for others than myself. (I must men-tion, however, that DuBois and Dewey have already laid a solid founda-tion for this task if only we would bring ourselves to take them seriously as *our intellectual ancestors*.)

Bibliography

Alexander, Michelle. *The New Jim Crow: Mass Incarceration in the Age of Colorblindness*. New York: The New Press, 2010.

Ambrose, Stephen. *The Victors: Eisenhower and His Boys*. New York: Simon and Schuster, 1999.

Beauchamp, Gorman. "Apologies All Around." *The American Scholar*, September 1, 2007. https://theamericanscholar.org/apologies-all-around/.

Bentham, Jeremy. *Colonies, Commerce, and Constitutional Law: Rid Yourselves of Ultramaria and Other Writings on Spain and Spanish America*. Edited by Philip Schofield. Oxford: Clarendon Press, 1995.

Brooks, David. "Giving Away Your Billion." *The New York Times*, June 6, 2017, Opinion. https://www.nytimes.com/2017/06/06/opinion/giving-away-your-billion-warren-buffett.html.

Cashin, Sheryll. *Place, Not Race: A New Vision of Opportunity in America*. Boston: Beacon Press, 2014.

Catron, Mandy Len. "To Fall in Love with Anyone, Do This (Updated With Podcast)." *The New York Times*, January 9, 2015, Fashion & Style: Modern Love. https://www.nytimes.com/2015/01/11/fashion/modern-love-to-fall-in-love-with-anyone-do-this.html.

Coates, Ta-Nehisi. *Between the World and Me*. New York: Spiegel & Grau, 2015.

———. "The Case for Reparations." *The Atlantic*, June 2014. https://www.theatlantic.com/magazine/archive/2014/06/the-case-for-reparations/361631/.

© The Editor(s) (if applicable) and The Author(s),
under exclusive licence to Springer International Publishing AG,
part of Springer Nature 2018
S. Rosenbaum, *Race, Justice and American Intellectual Traditions*,
https://doi.org/10.1007/978-3-319-76198-5

Conrad, Joseph. *Heart of Darkness*. Penguin Classics, edited by J. H. Stape. New York: Penguin Books, 2007.

Craig, Megan. *Levinas and James: Toward a Pragmatic Phenomenology*. Bloomington: Indiana University Press, 2010.

Curtin, Deane. *Chinnagounder's Challenge: The Question of Ecological Citizenship*. Bloomington: Indiana University Press, 1999.

Dewey, John. *The Collected Works of John Dewey*. Edited by Jo Ann Boydston. 3rd ed., 38 vols. Carbondale and Edwardsville: Southern Illinois University Press, 2008.

Dewey, John. *The Later Works, 1925–1953, Volume 7: 1932, Ethics*. Edited by Jo Ann Boydston. Carbondale, IL: Southern Illinois University Press, 1985.

Douglass, Frederick. *Narrative of the Life of Frederick Douglass, an American Slave*. Edited by John W. Blassingame, John R. McKivigan, Peter P. Hinks, and Gerald Fulkerson. New Haven, CT: Yale University Press, 2001.

DuBois, W. E. B. *The Souls of Black Folk*. Oxford World's Classics, edited by Brent Hayes Edwards. Oxford: Oxford University Press, 2007.

Emerson, Ralph Waldo. *Emerson's Essays*. New York: Harper Perennial, 1995.

Federal News Service. "Obama's Remarks at the Health Care Bill Signing." *The New York Times*, March 23, 2010, Politics. https://www.nytimes.com/2010/03/24/us/politics/24health-text.html.

Fernandez, Manny. "Federal Judge Says Texas Voter ID Law Intentionally Discriminates." *The New York Times*, April 10, 2017, U.S. https://www.nytimes.com/2017/04/10/us/federal-judge-strikes-down-texas-voter-id-law.html.

Freeman, Samuel. "Why Be Good?" *The New York Review of Books*, April 26, 2012. http://www.nybooks.com/articles/2012/04/26/why-be-good/.

Friedman, Milton. *Capitalism and Freedom*. Chicago: University of Chicago Press, 2002.

Gladwell, Malcolm. *Blink: The Power of Thinking Without Thinking*. New York: Little, Brown and Company, 2005.

Grimsrud, Ted. "Old Testament Justice (Amos)." *Peace Theology*, March 24, 2010. https://peacetheology.net/restorative-justice/5-old-testament-justice-amos/.

Hume, David. *A Treatise of Human Nature*. Edited by L. A. Selby-Bigge. Oxford: Clarendon Press, 1960.

Indian Summers. Drama, History, 2015. http://www.imdb.com/title/tt3706628/.

Kahneman, Daniel. *Thinking, Fast and Slow*. New York: Farrar, Straus and Giroux, 2011.

Krugman, Paul. "Understanding Republican Cruelty." *The New York Times*, June 30, 2017, Opinion. https://www.nytimes.com/2017/06/30/opinion/understanding-republican-cruelty.html.

Manicas, Peter T. "John Dewey and the Problem of Justice." *Journal of Value Inquiry* 15, no. 4 (1981): 279–91.

McIntyre, Alasdair. *After Virtue*. Notre Dame, IN: University of Notre Dame Press, 1981.

Mills, Charles W. "Rawls on Race/Race in Rawls." *The Southern Journal of Philosophy* 67 (2009): 161–84.

Mill, John Stuart. *On Liberty*. Edited by David Bromwich and George Kateb. New Haven: Yale University Press, 2003.

Newton, Isaac. *Philosophiae naturalis principia mathematica*. Edited by Alexandre Koyré and I. Bernard Cohen. 3rd ed. (1726). Cambridge, MA: Harvard University Press, 1972.

Nozick, Robert. *Anarchy, State, and Utopia*. New York: Basic Books, 1974.

Obergefell v. Hodges, No. 14-556 (Supreme Court of the United States June 26, 2015).

Parfit, Derek. *On What Matters*. 2 vols. Oxford: Oxford University Press, 2012.

Perry, Mark J. "Milton Friedman Interview from 1991 on America's War on Drugs." *American Enterprise Institute*, August 6, 2015. http://www.aei. org/publication/milton-friedman-interview-from-1991-on-americas-war-on-drugs/.

Plato. "Euthyphro." In *Plato: Complete Works*, edited by John M. Cooper, translated by G. M. A. Grube, 1–16. Indianapolis: Hackett, 1997.

———. "Laches." In *Plato: Complete Works*, edited by John M. Cooper, translated by Rosamond Kent Sprague, 664–86. Indianapolis: Hackett, 1997.

———. "Meno." In *Plato: Complete Works*, edited by John M. Cooper, translated by G. M. A. Grube, 870–97. Indianapolis: Hackett, 1997.

———. "Republic." In *Plato: Complete Works*, edited by John M. Cooper, translated by G. M. A. Grube and C. D. C. Reeve, 971–1223. Indianapolis: Hackett, 1997.

———. "Theaetetus." In *Plato: Complete Works*, edited by John M. Cooper, translated by M. J. Levett and Myles Burnyeat, 157–234. Indianapolis: Hackett, 1997.

Pratt, Scott. *Native Pragmatism*. Bloomington: Indiana University Press, 2002.

Rangel, Charles. Patient Protection and Affordable Care Act, Pub. L. No. H.R. 3950, 155–156 42 USC 18001 124 Stat. 119 (2010).

Rawls, John. *A Theory of Justice*. Cambridge, MA: Harvard University Press, 1971.

———. "The Obligation to Obey the Law." In *Morality and the Law*, edited by Robert M. Baird and Stuart Rosenbaum. Buffalo, NY: Prometheus Books, 1988.

———. *Political Liberalism*. The John Dewey Essays in Philosophy, no. 4. New York: Columbia University Press, 1993.

Rosenbaum, Stuart. *Pragmatism and the Reflective Life*. Lanham, MD: Lexington Books, 2009.

———. *Recovering Integrity: Moral Thought in American Pragmatism*. Lanham, MD: Lexington Books, 2015.

Sandel, Michael J. *Justice: What's the Right Thing to Do?* New York: Farrar, Straus and Giroux, 2009.

Smith, Alexander McCall. *Tears of the Giraffe*. New York: Anchor Books, 2002.

Stannard, David. *American Holocaust*. Oxford: Oxford University Press, 1992.

Stevenson, Bryan. *Just Mercy: A Story of Justice and Redemption*. New York: Spiegel & Grau, 2014.

Taylor, Pamela Ramsey. "Pamela Ramsey Taylor's Facebook Page." November 8, 2016.

Tocqueville, Alexis de. *Democracy in America*. Translated by Harvey C. Mansfield and Delba Winthrop. Chicago: University of Chicago Press, 2000.

Zemeckis, Robert. *Forrest Gump*. Comedy, Drama, Romance, 1994. http://www.imdb.com/title/tt0109830/.

Index